OUR GOLDEN RULE

Library of Congress Cataloging-in-Publications Data

McConnell, John H. - Author

Wengerd, Lori - Researcher

Browning, Amy - Cover Design

Our Golden Rule – 1st edt.

Includes Index

Library of Congress Control Number – 2004101091

ISBN 10: 1-931604-03-7 | ISBN 13: 978-1-931604-03-1

Franklin University Press

201 South Grant Avenue

Columbus, Ohio 43215-5399

614.947.6888

www.franklin.edu

leadership.franklin.edu

This book is dedicated to my wife, Peggy,
who put up with my travels and 80-hour work weeks.

Every year of our 58 years together
has been a joy.

OUR PHILOSOPHY

EARNINGS

The first corporate goal for Worthington Industries is to earn money for its shareholders and increase the value of their investment.

We believe that the best measurement of the accomplishment of our goal is consistent growth in earnings per share.

OUR GOLDEN RULE

We treat our customers, employees, investors and suppliers, as we would like to be treated.

PEOPLE

We are dedicated to the belief that people are our most important asset.

We believe people respond to recognition, opportunity to grow and fair compensation.

We believe that compensation should be directly related to job performance and therefore use incentives, profit sharing or otherwise, in every possible situation.

From employees we expect an honest day's work for an honest day's pay.

We believe in the philosophy of continued employment for all Worthington people.

In filling job openings every effort is expended to find candidates within Worthington, its divisions or subsidiaries.

CUSTOMERS

Without the customer and their need for our products and services we have nothing.

We will exert every effort to see that the customer's quality and service requirements are met.

Once a commitment is made to a customer, every effort is made to fulfill that obligation.

SUPPLIERS

We cannot operate profitably without those who supply the quality materials we need.

We ask that suppliers be competitive in the marketplace with regard to quality, pricing, delivery and volume purchased.

We are a loyal customer to suppliers who meet our quality and service requirements through all market conditions.

ORGANIZATION

We believe in a divisionalized organizational structure with responsibility for performance resting with the head of each operation.

All managers are given the operating latitude and authority to accomplish their responsibilities within our corporate goals and objectives.

In keeping with this philosophy, we do not create excessive corporate procedures. If procedures are necessary within a particular company operation, that manager creates them.

We believe in a small corporate staff and support group to service the needs of our shareholders and operating units as requested.

COMMUNICATION

We communicate through every possible channel with our customers, employees, shareholders, suppliers and financial community.

CITIZENSHIP

Worthington Industries practices good citizenship at all levels. We conduct our business in a professional and ethical manner.

We encourage all our people to actively participate in community affairs.

We support worthwhile community causes.

(Only <u>one</u> word has been changed since I wrote this more than 30 years ago.)

OUR GOLDEN RULE

"We treat our customers, employees, investors and suppliers as we would like to be treated."

(excerpted from "Our Philosophy" of Worthington Industries, by John H. McConnell)

OUR
GOLDEN
RULE

PROLOGUE

MR. MAC: A SPECIAL LEADERSHIP BASED ON RESPECT AND RECOGNITION

What's in a title? As the publishers of Mr. McConnell's book on leadership, we were given the difficult task of selecting a title. What word or phrase could capture the spirit of Mr. Mac? What title could convey his leadership? Above all, what title could make you, the reader, want to pick up this book and take it home?

Then it hit us: Those who know Mr. Mac won't be swayed by a title; you have come to respect the man on a different level. And those of you who get to know Mr. Mac through the pages of this book will realize there is no title that can truly capture his leadership, for it is entrenched in everything he does, every action he takes, every speech he gives.

Once you finish his book, you will understand how difficult it is for Mr. Mac to write about leadership. As he will tell you, he doesn't talk about the subject much, nor does he spend much time thinking about it. As those who have shared their views on Mr. Mac's leadership tell us, he just leads. He just "does it." Often he leads without the people who surround him realizing they are being led.

So then why the title, *Our Golden Rule*? Because the Golden Rule is a critical part of Worthington Industries' philosophy, captured on a 5-inch by 7-inch card with principles written by Mr. Mac more than 30 years ago. For you, the reader, this book will take you back to a simpler time when a common understanding of the Golden Rule led all business decisions. The title of this book will prepare you for the unique experience that awaits you: getting a glimpse of the spirit of Mr. John H. McConnell.

Enjoy!

Paul Otte, President of Franklin University
Lori Wengerd, Franklin University Press Researcher

"Worthington Industry's principles <u>can</u> be duplicated elsewhere.

While my father is one of the great leaders of our time,

he doesn't own the process."

JOHN P. McCONNELL
son of John H. McConnell and CEO of Worthington Industries

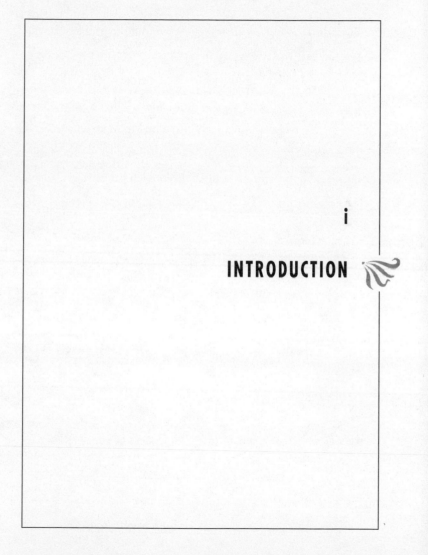

i

INTRODUCTION

INTRODUCTION

I often begin my speeches and papers with the story of my youth. I talk about my working class upbringing in West Virginia. I tell stories of my first eye-opening experience working in a manufacturing plant. I always describe how Worthington Industries went from a start-up company to the multibillion dollar, multifaceted public corporation it is today. But writing my thoughts on leadership is something I have not done before. It is an interesting process.

The topic of leadership isn't something I think about often. Although I am an avid reader, I tend to prefer biographies. Books on leadership aren't found among the collection in my den. I don't lecture on leadership, and I don't have a prepared response to questions about what is good or what is lacking in leadership today. As a matter of fact, when I was asked to write this book, I think I said "yes" too quickly, because the more I ruminate on my leadership style, the more I become convinced that I have nothing magical, extraordinary, or revolutionary to offer.

What you will find in this book is how a hard-working, trusting, loyal man from Pughtown, West Virginia, sees the world. You will get a

• MICK McDANIEL •

"John McConnell does the smartest thing in the world:

He listens to everybody, gets their input, then does

what he thinks is best. But believe me, there is a bit of

every conversation in the decisions he makes. Because

of his inclusive, decisive style, people don't even

realize they are being led. It's beautiful, really."

*Mick McDaniel was a schoolboy pal of John H. McConnell.
Their friendship was very close and complementary.
According to Mick, John was class vice president, pulling
guard on the football team, and pitcher on the baseball team.
Mick was class president, quarterback, and catcher. Both men
worked at Weirton Steel until Mick joined the Marine Corps.
After John joined the Navy, the two met unexpectedly in
Hawaii. Although they now live in different states,
they still talk on the phone several times a month and see
each other quite often. "It's frightening at times how well
we know each other," McDaniel adds.*

look at how I view the people in my life, from the employees who give their hearts and hands to Worthington Industries to the wife and friends from my youth whom I still cherish. If anything has happened to me in this writing process, it's that I have seen, in black and white, the absolutely vital role that *relationships* have in the life of this 80-something entrepreneur. Personally and professionally, I would not be who I am today if I had not responded to my own deep-rooted belief that the friendships I cherish and the people I help ultimately define me as a person.

Can leadership be learned? Most of it can. However, there is no magic formula to determine who the great leaders will be. I know that leaders cannot be measured by personality alone, for many types of temperaments can succeed. Leaders certainly can be measured on results, however. If their people produce, they are doing something right. This is how I knew that Donal Malenick was a leader. This is a man who started as a laborer with Worthington Steel Company and eventually became president. He was a doer, and with every successive position he held, his people were motivated and productive. No, Don and I are not alike. But we share one extremely important trait: a respect for people and an appreciation for the heart they put into their work.

In my opinion, every person who has a supervisory role in a company has an inherent *requirement* to be a leader.

• DONAL MALENICK •

"Our philosophy at Worthington Industries was to spend money on the customer in a bad economic cycle. And you know what? We always came out on top when the economy turned around. During recessionary times, we made serious capital expenditures: money was cheaper, we had confidence in the economy, we supported suppliers who also needed to stay in business, and we gave employees better tools to produce better product."

Donal Malenick served as president of Worthington Industries from 1976 until he retired in 1999. He also attended high school in West Virginia and is from a coal-mining family. He moved to Columbus and began working as a laborer for $1.66 an hour. For several years, Malenick was gone from Worthington, but returned in 1959, worked his way to president in 1976, and retired in 1999. "I didn't get this far on my own merit," Malenick likes to say. "A lot of people were by my side throughout my career."

A FUNDAMENTAL SHIFT
IS NEEDED

As I said earlier, I am not used to focusing on leadership alone. Most of my speeches revolve around the needs of corporations today. The word *leadership* is not in those speech notes, but the importance of having visionary, consistent, and visible and caring CEOs and officers underlies everything I believe.

In the 1980s, I began to suggest in my speeches that I saw four major problems with productivity in organizations: (1) lax management (which tends to happen in a strong market); (2) management teams that are no longer hands on; (3) a government that can be antagonistic to growth; and (4) unions that are much too adversarial. Fix these issues, and you fix America's business climate.

In economic downturns, corporate America has continually followed the path of least resistance. They immediately cut costs. What areas are affected first? Materials, R&D, capital spending, and manpower. The results are plummeting quality and inferior performance. How dare companies blame the American work ethic when corporate leaders re-

• DOUG MACLEAN •

"Nearly everyone who knows John McConnell knows
how he feels about the Golden Rule. The philosophy for
Worthington Industries has been to 'treat our customers,
employees, investors and suppliers as we would like to be
treated.' That philosophy is evident in the
Columbus Blue Jackets organization. From well-equipped locker
rooms to the team jet, the hockey players and staff
have visible evidence that Mr. Mac recognizes their
commitment to doing well. When asked about the reason
for the jet, Mr. Mac will tell people that hockey players
work hard, and loading them onto buses for overnight
trips doesn't recognize the family life they are
giving up while on the road."

*Doug MacLean is the first president and general manager
of the Columbus Blue Jackets ... the NHL team
founded and owned by John H. McConnell.*

*The Blue Jackets celebrated its first season
in Columbus, Ohio, in 2000.*

move all motivation for doing a good job and all potential for producing a good and desired product?

For management to affect a change in the way America's corporations operate, they first must make a commitment to recognize *people* as their most important asset. This includes improving incentives, building good profit-sharing programs, and capping executive pay and bonuses. Companies also must retain their innovative edge — but never at the expense of ethics.

☞

A WORD ABOUT "RECOGNITION"

Many companies hold annual recognition banquets that reward people for meeting their sales quotas. Some businesses recognize staff by sending them to meetings in far-flung cities. Others have nice newsletters that thank employees for their longevity. Those things are nice. People like to be noticed, thanked, and appreciated. We do those things at Worthington Industries, too.

However, I can't let readers go beyond this point without understanding what I mean when I say that *recognition* is the most important thing a CEO can do to build a company of strong, loyal employees. I am

• JOHN P. McCONNELL •

"I had an 'aha' moment one day when sitting next to my father on a plane. I asked him, 'What is more important, profit-sharing or recognition?' My dad looked at me and answered, 'Recognition, because that's what profit-sharing is all about.' Before that, I always thought he was talking about the pat-on-the-back side of recognition, but to him, recognition is much, much more. After that, I began to see clearly that my father had set up a company where employees are never treated as less than human."

John P. McConnell is CEO of Worthington Industries and son of Mr. Mac. He began working full time at Worthington Industries in 1975 doing shift work in the Louisville plant. In 1976, he began working in inside sales and, eventually, steel sales. He left the company for several years to serve as president of JMAC, the family investment company, and returned to Worthington Industries in 1992.

talking about the most vital trait any leader can have: the ability to *recognize* that every person in every department wants most of all to be seen as a human being with needs and desires that are not much different than his or her own. This was the basis for Jim Lincoln's management style at Lincoln Electric. Great leaders truly believe that the little things, such as a wave or a handshake, *do* matter, and the big things, such as decent pay and clean restrooms, make a difference in how hard people will work for them. If you don't honestly like people, if you don't empathize with others, and if you don't believe that all human beings are equal in the eyes of God and, therefore, should be valuable in the eyes of the CEO, there is nothing in this book that will work to make you a better leader.

Good leadership is all about *recognition*. Period. And this won't be the last time you read about it in my book.

THE PHILOSOPHY OF WORTHINGTON INDUSTRIES

As I said earlier, it is hard to separate the man from the company. My leadership skills that helped build this business (if that is what we need to call them for this book) have taken a life of their own. They can be seen

• BOB McCURRY •

"So many people have watched John's success. What

they have seen is a man who leads by example."

*Bob McCurry played football at Michigan State University from
1946 through 1950. He was center while John McConnell
played guard. From Pennsylvania, Bob is proud of the fact that
he also came from a humble background and moved on to
hold prominent positions in renowned corporations.
Bob worked for 28 years with Chrysler Corporation,
running the sales division before retiring. He held a similar
position at Toyota for another 12 years,
and still consults for the president of the company.*

*McCurry and McConnell have kept in touch often since they
met in the late 1940s. They both enjoy golf and meet when
possible to play a round at Double Eagle — McConnell's
private course in central Ohio.*

in the actions of every manager working here in every division, every department, and every office. When a company founder is as closely involved with day-to-day operations of the company as I was for many decades, every nook and cranny of the business has his fingerprint on it. The people I hired felt as I did. The people they hired shared our values, and so on and so on. After being part of this organization for only a short period of time, employees notice that we don't just talk about our beliefs, we live them.

Until I stepped down as operational head of the company and was not as able to walk as easily, I was involved with my employees. I walked the floors of the factories. I ate lunch with the foremen. At times, I even ran the machines when help was needed to fulfill an order. Therefore, my employees not only read memos that expressed my business philosophy, they also heard it from my very own mouth, and they saw how those philosophies could be put into action.

If you don't like getting your hands dirty or mingling with the troops, you don't need to read any further. No matter how good your personal philosophy may be, it won't ever become ingrained in the company unless you stand shoulder to shoulder with the men and women who make you successful.

About 30 years ago, I decided to put my basic philosophy in writ-

PEOPLE ORIENTED

People most important asset
 Compensation tied to people's
 efforts - Cash & Defferred P.S.

Salary Plan

Flex Benefits

Free Coffee & Haircuts

Open Door Policy

Non-Union in all operations
 except two acquired companies

PROFIT ORIENTED

Teach people what profit is -
 how to increase it

Extensive sales training

Quality & Service

Technical Service

MANAGEMENT STYLE

Golden Rule

No Policy Manual - Philoslphy
 on one page

No organization charts

Authority & Responsibility

No Committees

Small Corporate Staff

This is a scan of the laminated card I carry
in my breast pocket so that I am prepared when asked to make a speech.
I have used this same outline for more than 30 years.

ing and create a list of all of those beliefs that make Worthington Industries so successful. Because I had been living my beliefs, I didn't have to refer to textbooks, reread company newsletters, or pour over company personnel manuals. It didn't take more than an hour for me to compile this list. The words flowed onto the paper simply because those were words I spoke every day to anyone I happened to meet along the way. Today, that very same list still exists, but in a more formal way. It has been printed on a card entitled "Our Philosophy," which every employee has at his workstation and every division has hanging in its lobbies. This 5" x 7" card contains only 371 words, but every phrase matters, and the employees understand their meaning. I carry this card in my breast pocket, even though I know what it says by heart.

Notice that the title on the card is "Our Philosophy," not "Company Philosophy," "The Philosophy of Worthington Industries," or "Words of Wisdom from the CEO." Use of the word *our* is significant. I never felt that cramming the philosophy down the throats of our employees would work. We don't ever say to them, "Here is a card that lists everything we expect from you. Memorize it." Instead, employees know before joining the company or before encouraging friends and relatives to work for us that if they don't share the same beliefs, they shouldn't bother asking to be part of the team.

Those words I penned more than 30 years ago haven't changed to this day. We don't operate our company based on the leadership trend of the month. We don't change philosophies at the whim of the board of directors or the demands of the customer. The way in which Worthington Industries operates today is consistent with the founding principles that allowed it to grow. Therefore, it is no coincidence that the men and women on the factory floor today demonstrate the same desire to put in an honest day's work as the men who worked the machines in 1955. Our employees do not need to guess at how their bosses will react to ideas, requests, and remarks because they understand why Worthington Industries is in business. This consistency of philosophy has carried our company through the extreme ups and downs of the 20th-century steel industry. Not only are we stronger for it today, we are the only steel company that is strong enough to consistently retain the loyalty of our stockholders.

THE TOP 100 BEST COMPANIES TO WORK FOR
Fortune Magazine • 2004
"No time clocks in these steel-processing plants. Workers get profit-sharing payouts ranging from 40% to 70% of base pay, and the company pays 100% of health insurance premiums for employees and family members."

1

COMMUNICATION

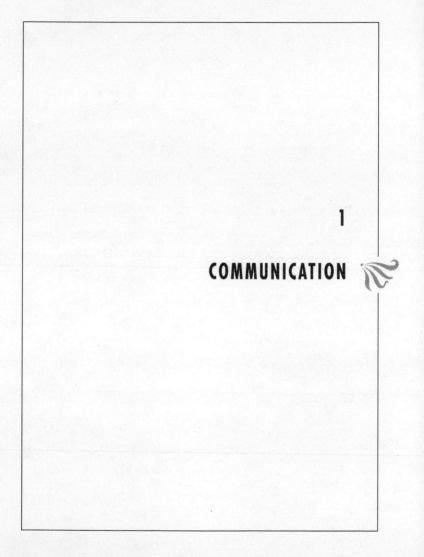

KEEPING IT SIMPLE

Although I served for many years on the Board of Directors for Wendy's International, I still like to quote an old friend, Ray Kroc, the founder of McDonald's. Every time Mr. Kroc was asked to give his secret to success, he worked the following words into his answer: "Keep it simple." In our industrial world, where unions are prominent and lawyers sit by our side at every important meeting, this KIS philosophy is not always easy to carry out, but I won't back down.

One of the main goals of all leaders — whether or not they have read the major textbooks on leadership philosophy — is to motivate employees to work hard and make the right decisions. If you are not motivating people to do the right thing for the right reason, you are not leading them.

In order to motivate employees, every CEO develops incentive programs. Some of those programs involve pay, some involve benefits, others involve travel rewards, and most involve a clear view of the opportunities for advancement. I have seen company leaders craft these marvelous plans that involve sliding pay scales for production quotas. I have been asked to review sales-incentive programs that give prizes for every milestone reached. Yes, some have been creative, and some have actually worked. However, none of them were effective in motivating employees unless they were, first and foremost, *simple*.

When I talk of simplicity, I am referring to the program itself *and* to the communication of it. Sliding scales that require employees to use algebraic calculations to understand how they will benefit just will not work. From the first year of The Worthington Steel Company, we had an incentive program of some sort. In the beginning, this program was based on tons of steel shipped, which was very effective in encouraging high productivity. This incentive was paid in cash in a separate check sealed with the employees' regular paychecks.

Eventually, our steel production became much more complex, making it hard to equate tonnage with profitability. At that time, in 1966, we changed our incentive plan from straight tonnage to bottom-line profit. We tied the payout to salary so that each employee would have an incentive to improve his or her position in the company. We then decided to pay in cash, rather than in benefits or stocks. With a group of young employees on the front lines and in our offices, we knew that a deferred plan would not generate the day-to-day productivity we were looking to develop. Our employees appreciated cash above all else.

The noise that we made in the industry by sharing our profits with employees was deafening. Unions hated profit-sharing because it put labor in bed with management. Other companies couldn't believe we wanted to reward non-management employees with profits they believed were created solely by management decisions. Obviously, we helped change the way companies think about profit-sharing, and I'm proud of that.

The programs we have developed over the years would not have been effective if they were not *simple*. Unless employees see a direct correlation between contribution and reward, the program doesn't make sense. In our business, we have employees who hold MBAs and understand how to read even the most complex financial statement. We also have people in our plants who have not earned a high school diploma. It is just as important for our line people to understand the incentive program as it is for our management to be able to explain it to them.

Simplicity in communication requires us to think carefully about how we word our memos and newsletters. More importantly, simplicity means that every supervisor at every level of the company understands the incentive program and is able to answer the questions that arise on a daily basis. Both informal and formal lines of communication must be clear and easy, which means that a good leader has a hand in controlling the message, as well.

• JOHN P. McCONNELL •

"Of course we're different, my father and me.

But having been part of Worthington Industries for so

long, I hold the same values upon which my father

founded the company: keep it simple, count on clarity,

tell the truth, and give good direction.

I look at 'Our Philosophy' and realize that core values

don't change. And I realize that these are

great principles for life ... not just for business.

People have a hard time when they try to live one way

at home and bring a separate self to work."

❦

THE ROLE OF SUPERVISORS

No matter how hard I worked as CEO to develop rapport with clients or create incentive programs for employees, none of my plans would have moved very far beyond the head office without help from the supervisors under me. Think about the age-old game of Telephone. A very simple message could be passed easily from one player to the next without being changed by the time it reached the end of the line. A more complex message, however, would be misquoted and misunderstood with every pair of ears that heard it and every pair of lips that spoke it, until the final player had absolutely no understanding of the original message. Like that game, the role of the supervisor as the next person in line is a vital consideration for every business model.

Not every message can be simplified, and it is not important that complex issues be repeated verbatim by the last person in line. What does matter is that the essence of the message makes it to the end of the line. For that to happen, everyone in line must understand the philosophies of the leader and be committed to keeping the sum and substance of the message intact. *That* is the role of the supervisor. If you, as a leader, expect your philosophy to move beyond your office walls, then you must do two things: (1) make sure that the people down the line from you understand where you are coming from and that they share those beliefs; and (2) take time to step into the middle of the line once in a while to help move the correct message along.

This second point does not mean that I believe in overriding the decisions of the supervisors whom I have entrusted at all levels. For the most part, I do not condone this kind of intervention. There is a difference, however, between talking to employees about day-to-day operational matters (which is the role of the supervisor) and having contact with employees at all levels in order to listen to their needs and impart words of advice that reflect the company philosophy. In order to have a winning game of Telephone, you must step into the middle of the line once in a while to make sure the message is being well taken care of.

Here is another reason why breakdowns occur in this vital game of Telephone: One of the players in the middle of the line wants to mix up the game a bit. This person views his turn at Telephone as an opportunity to "make a difference." We all know someone who fancies himself a renegade. I am not afraid to say that these employees are dangerous to an organization that has plans for longevity and success. No matter how often leaders say they want to embrace people who have new ideas and better ways, leaders also expect those ideas to move through the proper channels and be implemented at the right time, if at all. Today, too many companies say they will reward the "cowboy" without providing the right forum for recording, studying, and implementing new ideas. After 48 years of watching a company grow, I can tell you that the person who changes the message as it passes through him is *not* moving the company forward. That person is *not* helping his people be part of the larger team. Leaders who allow renegades to mix things up are putting the integrity of the company at stake. The self-serving individual has no place in a company where teamwork is a top priority.

The role of the supervisor, then, is twofold: (1) to listen for questions and seek solutions by moving the problem up the line to the point where it can be fixed, and (2) to make sure that the underlying and very basic philosophy of the leadership is taken to heart and carried out by each and every employee in his care.

AN OPEN DOOR POLICY MEANS JUST THAT

Many leaders today *say* they have an open door policy. Then, the CEO will actually leave his door wide open during business hours and claim he

• DONAL MALENICK •

"I'll bet it's hard for Mr. Mac to write this book because his leadership style is hard to define. It is the most unique style I have ever seen. He got out of the way and allowed people to take responsibility and use authority. He was always looking to promote, not fire. He was firm but fair. And while he was demanding, he wouldn't ask anyone to do something he wouldn't do himself."

has done his job. At Worthington Industries, supervisors at every level understand that their jobs are to encourage two-way communication with their employees, but we do a better job than by just propping open the office door.

If building a *strong* company requires playing an airtight game of Telephone, I submit that building a *highly productive company* requires a way to propel ideas back up the chain of command. Time and again, I have heard suggestions from the plant floor that have revolutionized our business. Employees who work the machines have given ideas for cutting production time, improving products, and saving on materials. People in accounts payable have shared plans for saving money with our suppliers. Janitors have voiced concerns that improved working conditions for hundreds of employees. No solid company today believes that the only worthy ideas come from the top. But moving those ideas from the floor to the front office is not always a part of a company's culture.

In a company like Worthington Industries that has so many employees and a reputation for listening to them, there is a protocol for handling comments and ideas. The supervisor of a plant in the Midwest needs to know that his idea may not make it to the boardroom level, but he must feel that the people just above him will care enough to listen.

When I say "open door policy," I mean that access to supervisors must be unhindered. When people in our company agree to take on a supervisory role, they know they are agreeing not just to hand down punishment and rewards, but also to keep the company sparkling with new life and better methods. We don't expect supervisors to come up with all the ideas themselves, but we do count on them to open their doors — and their minds — to new ideas.

Our supervisors also understand that better ways of operating often come to them in the form of complaints. Not every employee has the capacity to develop solutions for each situation, but those who are concerned enough to approach a supervisor with a legitimate problem should be thanked for bringing the complaint forward. True, some complaints are not valid, and the employee must be told that. Other complaints can be handled only if the supervisor is smart enough to know that his own boss is the best person to handle the situation. And when that happens, the open door policy comes into play again.

Supervisors must be well informed because the people who work for them expect answers. That said, I also realize that no one makes the best decisions 100% of the time, and we don't fault our supervisors when they make a wrong decision. Sometimes, they turn away an idea or avoid a complaint too quickly, without giving proper thought to it. Recognizing that sometimes hearing "no" is not good enough for the employee who has a valid complaint or grand idea, I made a commitment from the very start that every employee has the right to see me or another officer about any issue that is on his mind.

That philosophy has paid off. Over the years, dozens of people have asked to schedule an appointment with me. Sometimes, their supervisors are included so I can hear both sides of the issue. While every meeting has not ended with the employee having his or her way, every meeting has made a difference in the company. Those open door meetings help me keep in touch with real, gut-wrenching decisions that are made every day on the front line. They also allow me to meet employees I may not have met on my plant visits. Most importantly, however, these meetings have helped me identify leadership potential in some of the people who have been gutsy enough to go straight to the top.

I remember one couple who came to see me years ago. They called to make an appointment, and drove several hours to meet with me in my Worthington office. "What's on your mind?" I asked them. They told me, "You're forcing us to live in sin." As it turned out, our policy against allowing married couples to work for us was keeping this man and woman from tying the knot. Neither one of them wanted to quit. The result of that meeting was a policy change for our organization that still stands today, allowing plant supervisors to set rules about married couples. Good

• DONAL MALENICK •

"While every employee knew we expected them

to go through the chain of command with problems

or ideas, they also knew that Mr. Mac and I were

available to them. All the managers had

our home phone numbers and addresses,

and we did get calls after hours at home."

for those two people for taking the time to go straight to the top. And good for our company because we don't forget that some seemingly small issues actually can matter very much to someone else.

Open door policies are the only way to keep management fresh and employees satisfied.

☞

WITHOUT FOLLOW-UP, NOTHING MATTERS

Have you ever proposed a great idea only to have it fall into the great abyss of apathy? To you, perhaps yours was a revolutionary idea. To the person who killed it, it would have been an albatross around the organization's neck. Still, you would have appreciated knowing what people thought about your idea. Maybe it was discredited within five minutes, or maybe your idea sparked a two-hour discussion at the last board meeting. If you didn't know the reaction you caused, you would have no motivation to come forward again.

At this point, I am adding one more important responsibility for great leaders: follow-up. It is always tough for me when employees stop me in the plant to ask about the status of a project they recommended.

Occasionally, I have been caught off guard because I didn't have enough information to answer their questions. But someone should have followed-up with them. Why, I wanted to know, didn't the supervisor ever get back to this poor fellow who stuck his neck out for the company?

It doesn't take much to be good at follow-up. If a proposal is still under consideration, then the people involved need to know that it has not been turned down. If a complaint was determined to be unjustified, the person who initiated it should be told why nothing could be done. Sometimes, employees want to take the idea to the next level ... and that's their right. When ideas or suggestions have merit, the originator should be congratulated. I cannot think of a good reason that follow-up should not be done. Nothing can dampen the spirit of an employee more than being encouraged to walk through "open doors," then being ignored.

I know, I know. Chronic complainers do exist in the halls of every business. Should these people be listened to *every* time? Absolutely. A wise supervisor, however, will find a way to tame the complaints. Perhaps he asks for all of them to be submitted in writing. That might solve the problem. I have seen supervisors put "chronic complainers" in charge of finding a solution, only to discover a natural-born leader among the ranks.

Whether the employee is coming to you or your managers with ideas, complaints, suggestions, recommendations, or praise, to not follow-up sends a message that input is not wanted. And nothing can kill the spirit of a business faster than that.

☞

AN EMPLOYEE COUNCIL FOR TRUE COMMUNICATION

In a short amount of time, The Worthington Steel Company grew so large that I was not able to have regular, personal contact with all employees or even all supervisors. With a strong desire to stay in touch with front-line workers, and looking for a way to show my respect for the opinions of everyone who worked for the company, I formed an Employee Council. This group was structured to help with two-way communication and motivate employees who wanted to be involved. The program still exists today. Originally, the people who sat on the Employee Council were hand-picked by management to ensure that we would have people around the table who were respected by both us and their fellow employees. The members of the committee rotated on and off according to a set schedule, with committee members selecting their own replacements. A member of management chaired the meeting, and I often joined the group to hear first hand the issues of the day. Very little

• MICK McDANIEL •

"I visited plants with Mr. Mac and saw how people always knew his name; when he couldn't walk as well, they got him a golf cart and he'd load it up with cold drinks and deliver them. John's way is time-consuming. He took breaks from the mental processes to do physical things like visit plants. Human relationships always come first, which is why he is so admired."

about that original committee structure has changed.

Today, those committees continue to meet every month and serve as a valuable tool for communications and progress reports. All employees know where to turn to make sure someone addresses their complaints and puts forth recommendations for improvements to quality, production, and working conditions. Every question that comes from the Employee Council to management is answered. Every one of them.

Perhaps the most important role the councils play is their input in the hiring process. Even today, every employee is hired under a probationary period. For those three months, new employees work side-by-side with those who observe the new person's commitment and work ethic. Employee councils take peer input into consideration when it comes time to grant full-time employment — or not grant it. In an environment like a steel plant, where one man counts so heavily on another, the issue of "fitting in" becomes extremely important. If employees don't trust the person next to them who is running the controls for the machine they stick their hands under, the team structure breaks down.

Because we do try in our hiring process to assess the level that each applicant seems to share our company's values, new hires usually are very good. Occasionally, however, the councils do stop the full hiring of an individual, and we are grateful for that. These councils take full responsibility for the decision.

There is another benefit to having an employee council: Having an open door management policy does not guarantee employees will use it. Some people will never feel comfortable speaking to management, no matter what you do to encourage them. They probably grew up with high expectations for respecting authority — and they make good employees. However, these same people will open up to peers and come forward with great suggestions. For this reason, the Employee Councils allow us to get input from many more people than we would otherwise.

✄

YOU DON'T NEED TO SAY ANYTHING TO COMMUNICATE

I am not a very quotable man. You won't find part of my speeches in Bartlett's collection of memorable sayings. I admire Will Rogers, but don't share his ability for poignant quips. In my life, I have met many men who can talk a good talk. My friend Mick McDaniel is one of them. On the other hand, I can name other men who have a sharp wit, but don't offer much else in the way of leadership. They sound good at the podium, but can't seem to move ideas beyond the boardroom.

Have you ever met someone who impressed you with his salesmanship? He said the right thing, made the right gestures, closed the deal when he should have. Sometimes, these people are indeed very effective when they return to the office. Other times, you realize their promises are hollow and their follow-up is absent. That's not how any leader should want to be remembered.

Communication is an absolutely vital trait for excellent leadership, without a doubt. However, don't think for a second that good speaking skills equate to good communication skills.

Just ask my employees. When talking about me, most of them can't repeat funny phrases I uttered or a particularly pithy bit of advice I offered. They will, however, tell you a story about how I came to see them one Saturday morning in the plant and put on bib overalls to help finish the job so everyone could go home. They will tell you how the quality care at our health center saved their lives, and the affordability of our health care saved their families from bankruptcy. People go out of their way to show me their new haircuts from the Worthington Industries' barbershop. Young employees run across the floor to shake my hand and tell me how the recent profit-sharing check allowed them to buy their first home. These are the ways in which great leaders communicate.

My office overlooks the plants at our Worthington, Ohio, site.

• BOB McCURRY •

"John and I both believe that when you

begin to rely on computers, you lose touch with people.

John grew such a strong organization because

he relied on personal contact and didn't expect

computers to tell him what to do."

One time, after showing our new General Counsel to his corner office with a view of the sprawling expanse of Columbus, I noticed a funny look on his face. He didn't want to say anything, but after I prompted him to tell me what was on his mind, he said, "I don't think I should have an office with a nicer view than yours. Would you like to take this opportunity to trade?" But I would rather face the factories, I told him. To me, the only view that is valuable is one that gives me a sense of how my employees are doing. As I gaze out my office window, I feel connected. That, to me, is communication; and it has nothing to do with words.

☞

FORGET ANYTHING
BUT WORD OF MOUTH

I have e-mail, voice-mail, and an answering machine or two. I use the telephone quite a bit, just like any businessman. I enjoy reading newsletters from the companies in which I am involved. But no method is as important to me as having a conversation, face-to-face, with another human being.

Look at any employee survey conducted by your company or others. The number one issue that troubles employees is *communication*. It

• DONAL MALENICK •

"Mr. Mac always was good at asking questions.
If I didn't have the answer, I'd be sure to find out
before his next visit. When I became president,
I worked across the hall from Mr. Mac. If both of us
were in the office, we would chat every day,
several times a day. We had very few closed-door
meetings between us. From those brief
but frequent encounters, I learned to do many things
just because they were the right thing to do."

doesn't matter if you hang a weekly newsletter in the lunchroom, send a video message from the president every month to every office, or maintain a Web site for employees. It still comes down to the fact that people are hungry for information that comes from the mouths of their bosses.

What do they want to know? Many employees do care about the company's financial situation. They are interested in reading about the latest list of new clients. Some people like to know about policy changes or see who among them is celebrating a wedding or a new baby. However, your employees are most concerned about their place in the company, how their work is being perceived, the equipment they are using, the schedule for the upcoming week, and the impact that the year-end financial statements will have on their profit-sharing checks. These workers aren't selfish; they are just like you and me. They want to know, first and foremost, whether or not their job is secure. Once they feel comfortable with that knowledge, their minds are open to hearing other information.

Think about what I just said. If your employees' main concerns are about matters relating to them personally, they won't find that information in the company newsletter. No matter how many ways you communicate with them, or how packed full of information your newsletter is, employees crave contact that confirms their role in the work world. And only a direct supervisor can provide that information. A good leader understands this basic desire for information, understands how information can relate to a sense of security, and encourages the kind of personal-contact communication that keeps a company humming.

Too many managers today are relying on e-mail and voice-mail to move information through the company. Sometimes it is easier to send an e-mail to multiple people than it is to visit that many offices. Sometimes, that's fine. However, we all have been surprised by an e-mail that sounds too harsh or a voice-mail message that is misunderstood. And electronic conversations lack depth. They don't encourage the meatier back-and-forth discussion that often brings the best decision. As much as people appreciate hearing the bad news in person, they also like to hear the good news in person from someone higher up than they are. That conversation is something they will cherish forever.

I can say with confidence that I do not know one good leader who stays in his office more than he is talking to others. All good leaders make the effort each day to interact with as many different departments as possible. They don't delegate their role as chief communicator, and they realize their greatest power lies in their ability to motivate simply by looking in the eyes of their employees.

EXPECT UP AND DOWN COMMUNICATION

Just as great CEOs are the chief communicators of the company, supervisors at every level need to understand that unless they are spending a good portion of their time talking to their people, listening to their people, and reporting to their bosses, they don't need the title of supervisor.

I am a firm believer that supervisors and managers must be doers and motivators. No matter how good they may be at completing quality and timely projects, that doesn't automatically qualify them for a leadership role. I have seen excellent employees fail at being supervisors. Perhaps these men and women are fast, productive, smart, reliable, and innovative. If you ask them to draw up the work schedule, they'll do a great job. If you need them to recommend the next equipment purchase, their research and report will be outstanding. Sometimes, however, these same people are not meant to supervise. A funny thing happens when you put these people in charge of others: They aren't happy. It is not a natural role for them, and they would rather be successful.

What this means, of course, is that companies must have ways to reward workers other than putting them in charge of people. Only those

• DONAL MALENICK •

"What always struck me as odd about Worthington

Industries was how few policies were in place.

We had such high expectations for communication that

everyone understood what was required of him or her

... and why. Every supervisor knew they were being

paid partly to carry messages up and down the chain of

command. Like Mr. Mac, I strongly believed that

nothing beats TALKING to each other. It was amazing

what I would learn by sitting down with a couple of

guys in the company cafeteria."

who can communicate well and care enough to make sure the messages move up and down the chain of command should be in charge of others.

Although most supervisors understand their role in working with the people they supervise directly, some of them forget that the company leaders need to hear from them, as well. The communication they are charged with must go up the ladder as often as it moves down. Supervisors must be encouraged to share information, and it must be made known to them that the CEO relies on their message in this game of Telephone.

Looking back at all the wonderful men and women who have worked with me over the years, I have great memories of the faces of the many supervisors as they sat across the table from me, delighting in the successes of their people. Nothing made my day more enjoyable than having a department head schedule a meeting with me just to share a milestone the entire department had reached together. When those supervisors would share an idea from a new employee or would tell me how their departments were improving production because of a new machine we purchased, it validated everything I believed in. You see, a good leader does not only want to be part of major decisions. A good leader also wants to revel in the small successes of the smallest department.

I often reflect on the excitement that filled the department when a supervisor returned from my office to tell everyone, "I let Mr. Mac know about such and such, and he wants to share his hearty congratulations." Supervisors who care enough to move a message up — and back down — the chain of command tell employees that their efforts were noticed. In turn, those same people take pride in their work and feel more connected to the organization. After I learned about such an accomplishment in a particular plant or department, I would follow-up with a visit to congratulate the people myself. If I were unable to do that within a reasonable amount of time, I would send a hand-written note to the team. There is no doubt that the note was posted on the lunchroom wall and everyone who saw it knew I was aware of their hard work.

True leaders find joy in recognizing small accomplishments — and they can only hear about these achievements if communication up and down the chain is expected and carried out.

2

INVOLVED MANAGEMENT

☞

MANAGEMENT IS NOT A SCIENCE

I don't expect this book to be used as a teaching tool in business schools throughout the nation. It lacks formulas and self-assessment tools and quotable "Rules for Success." But I'm fine with that. I have never believed that management is a science that could be defined and pulled apart and summarized in a checklist.

Simply put, spend too much time thinking about how you should manage and you certainly are not taking the time to manage. I say, "Just do it." To every business management student, I suggest that you simply believe in the Golden Rule, then live by it. *Do unto others as you would have them do unto you.*

Good leaders are able to look into the eyes of the people who are working for them. They see beyond their desktops and enjoy the people much more than they enjoy financial statements or production quotas or pending orders. They know that to make a company successful, it takes human beings who have families that love them — people who want to walk across the threshold at the end of the day holding their heads high because they put in a hard day's work and were appreciated for it. My point is this: The intention behind the Golden Rule is as important as carrying it out. From the time I was 10, I had a job. Always a intent observer of human nature, I understood even then that people produce better if they are treated well. Everyone knows that the Golden Rule works for spouses and families and friends. Why wouldn't it hold true for our jobs?

With pages of numbers to back me up, I can prove that an excellent work environment increases your chance for success. It allows for better products, less waste, more innovation, and superior customer service. Just look at how far Worthington Industries has come from an office in the basement of my first home to this. Yet, while I feel that happy employees do impact my company's profitability, that's only a side benefit of treating people well. I feel deeply that people should be treated well not because they are *tools* for building a successful company, but because they are valuable as human beings. I have met hollow leaders who think they have good relationships with people when, in fact, they are treating them like nothing more than pawns in their personal game of chess. Those leaders are good at making all people feel like they are part of the game … for a while. Then people begin to see through them, understanding that pawns will be sacrificed to save the king and queen. From that point on, the leadership becomes ineffective and operates more like a dictatorship. Inevitably, the company begins a downhill slide.

There is no science to management. There is no standard pattern of successful leaders. If you think so, you will spend more time trying to perfect your scientific formula than in simply leading your company proudly into the future. My best advice is to wake up each day committing yourself to lead by example and to act in the same ethical, hard-working manner you expect from your employees.

When I saw supervisors who were faltering, I reminded them that it's time to become involved with their people again. Most of the time, a manager who is losing control of his or her team is also losing touch with that team. It's time to eat lunch with employees in order to reconnect with them on a personal level. That manager should walk the floor a little more often and take time to ask how a process is working or how a machine is performing. When supervisors are involved with their people instead of being involved only with their paperwork, they not only *feel* more effective, they *are* more effective.

So that's all the science I can offer: Live by the Golden Rule; be involved; lead by example. My formula does not offer any of the "input" measurements that scientists like to see, but my way gets results.

• TOM PETERS •

excerpt from Thriving on Chaos

"All quality control at Worthington Industries

is done by the operators, who have the latest

measurement equipment to aid them. They also do

all except the major maintenance, having wholesale

access to unlocked parts and tool rooms.

All salespeople train extensively on the machines.

Sales reviews are held on the shop floor regularly.

Order information is available to all."

☞

RIGHT PEOPLE
IN THE RIGHT PLACES

Not everyone is cut out to be a CEO. Some of the best leaders I have known understand that they are far more effective as chief financial officer or vice president of human resources than they ever could be in running an entire operation. Leaders don't have to rise to "the top" to be important to the company's success.

As CEO, one of the most vital roles I played was to recognize talent and make sure it was being used to its fullest potential. It is possible for someone in sales to have skills that are better suited for the distribution department, and unless leaders are good at putting the right people in the right positions, they lose their effectiveness as leaders.

Because we set our standards for hiring so high, I always have been confident in the people we bring to Worthington Industries. By having such a desirable company to work for, one that has been recognized by many corporate pundits and proven by our low turnover rate, we have encouraged a nice flow of applicants. Even in the toughest employment markets, we never had to worry about having a good pool of people from which to hire. By bringing in good people, half the battle of

• BOB McCURRY •

"John has an uncanny ability to hire the right people.

He attracts people who are like him, and he's good

about spotting the ones who are a good fit for the

organization and bringing them along.

John is a great producer and a never-ending worker,

and the people he hires are just like him."

retaining good employees is won.

With the Employee Council I described before, Worthington Industries has been able to identify early on those people who didn't fit well with our company's philosophy. This process of (1) having the best candidates to choose from and (2) not allowing destructive personalities to stay with the corporation has given us an excellent group of employees, allowing us to promote heavily from within our own walls.

Sometimes, having the right people in the right place means matching talents with the skills needed in a particular job. Good supervisors are able to recognize that one hard-working, dependable employee who isn't keeping up with a task can be successfully moved to another post. A good leader, however, also recognizes that moving people around and promoting them to positions that stretch their abilities can build an excellent base of generalists who will make better leaders because they have been exposed to many facets of the company.

Another benefit that comes with moving people into different positions is that new ideas often emerge. A top accounting employee may see something completely different in the production process if he or she is invited to be part of another team. When you have good people, you can trust that they can be good at more than one task.

If there is any area where people have found fault with me, it's the

• JOHN P. McCONNELL •

"I think it's important to create an environment
where you can get honest input and fresh viewpoints.
Sometimes we get that by hiring from outside,
but it also happens by moving people around within
the company. My father was always moving
the right people into the right places."

fact that I have a hard time letting people go when they need to go. When people show loyalty to the company, I like to give them perhaps too many chances to perform. Fortunately, I was able to hire people who were better at cutting ties with unproductive workers than I was.

In the past 10-15 years, the growth of the company has been such that Worthington Industries has found it necessary to hire some key personnel from outside the organization. Still, the tendency to search for a good fit from within the company remains.

☞

EVERY MANAGER NEEDS PASSION

Nothing is quite so obvious to employees as a manager who is only going through the motions. Once I see a supervisor who lacks passion, I know he can no longer deliver the level of work we expect.

It's easy to recognize passionate supervisors. They are hungry for information. They search out answers for their questions and the questions of those who work for them. A passionate supervisor lights up when one of his bosses comes into view because he wants to show off a new piece of equipment or talk about an idea for improving the process. He is the first one to read the company newsletter and discuss parts of it with his employees. He is confident about presenting solutions at division meetings or passing a bit of news to the head office. Most importantly, a passionate manager is contagious. His staff reflects that enthusiasm and is eager to put in a good hard day's work. I would not trade passion for any other trait.

Can a good leader instill passion? Absolutely, by being passionate himself. Show me a CEO who loves the company he is with, enjoys the big decisions as much as the small accomplishments, believes in his product, and appreciates his people, and I'll show you an inspiring leader. Although you might not find the word "passion" in every leadership book you pick up, the presence of passion is inferred. Think of Abraham Lincoln or Ronald Reagan, Martin Luther King, Jr. or Bill Gates. It's obvious to everyone that such men have passion for their work.

When a CEO or a supervisor loses passion, it's time to move on. For a supervisor, that can mean moving to another department or taking on a different role. For a CEO, that means leaving an organization to make room for somebody who can feel the same passion he once did.

Can a good leader kill passion? Of course. And that often is what causes companies to begin the spiral downward. Sometimes, a leader can fake passion, especially when a company is doing well. He can smile easily at the right time, use words of encouragement, whistle in the hallways, and pat people on the back. Then, at the first downturn, the lack of passion is exposed, serving as a catalyst for failure. The smiles turn to looks of panic, and the pats on the back turn to finger pointing. The whistling turns into words of blame. Why? Because that leader never believed in the product or the team of employees as much as he believed in the bottom line.

Passion can pull a company through any complex issue or economic uncertainty. Passion leads to innovation. Passion is irreplaceable.

☞

FINANCIALS ARE NOT THE FINAL WORD

Our stockholders are important to Worthington Industries. These are the people who have voted for us with their wallets. And because we have proven our consistency and fortitude, they have continued to prove their loyalty to us. To stockholders, and to many of the officers on our board of directors, the financial statements of the company are everything. They use the numbers to judge our company's health and potential. Depending on their knowledge of numbers, these observers also use financial statements to think they can help us make decisions. I don't have the same interest in the financial statements. To me, they are a review of where our company has been. By looking at last quarter's numbers, I can tell a good deal about profitability and runaway expenses. However, I already know most of the information that our corporate officers learn from the numbers. I expect the people at every level of supervision to know, on a daily basis, how sales are trending, how much the cost of materials is increasing, how much inventory we have, and how much difference we are seeing in labor costs due to increased or decreased production. CEOs that live and die by the numbers are creating a company that holds its breath every month until those CEOs have time to dissect the financials and send down edicts from the top. On the other hand, CEOs who are involved in the management of the company and have open relationships with their managers can make decisions on a daily basis that impact the month-end numbers. And their supervisors don't hold their breath. They understand that a well-timed warning about increasing costs or a slight increase in productivity can be addressed before it becomes a problem or a warning sign for the investors.

In short, financial statements are a look back at what was. In a proactive company that makes hard decisions daily, the numbers can change dramatically by the next month's release because the people in charge don't have to wait until the 10th of the month to make a decision.

To our stockholders and board members, however, being involved in day-to-day operations is impossible. The financial statements, then, are important for keeping those interested parties informed about the company's progress. But allowing decisions to be made from financial statements without an accompanying report of what has been addressed to date is not an effective way to run a company.

At Worthington Industries, we do share financial information with our employees. With a profit-sharing plan in place, it's important for employees to understand where their investments are headed and be able to react quickly to improve the profitability. However, it's very important to choose the information that best conveys the financial status of the company. Not every line item is relevant. By the same token, it's also important to select the best way to convey the financial information. We rely on several means to tell our story, not just one.

Yes, numbers are important, but the leader who is surprised by a line item in the monthly statement is a leader who has lost track of his contact points in the company. If the sales numbers are a surprise, you need to reconnect with your VP of sales. If expenses seem out of control, your purchasing department and plant managers need to know that you expect more reporting. Today's surprises should be a wake-up call.

When leaders can get to the position where the numbers are sim-

• JOHN P. McCONNELL •

"We are measured every day in the
New York Stock Exchange. I know exactly what's
expected of me; the trick is to let everyone else
know about those expectations. I also see my job
as preparing the next leadership, and to go
when it's time to go."

ply verification of what they already know, then the financial department becomes only necessary in an advisory role, not as a decision-making body. Leaders need their financial wizards to help them decipher the impact of decisions, but not to make the decisions. They need their CFO to recommend ways to refigure the accrual system, but not to advise on cutting the cost of materials. These decisions should be left up to the department that knows best. I have seen many companies suffer from an overbearing finance and accounting office instead of allowing decisions to be made at a more appropriate level. Don't let this happen to you.

☞

OK, THERE IS A FORMULA

Those of you who still are looking for a magic potion from me, here is the best I can do: Good management is 80% people orientation; 15% learned skills; 5% gut feel.

Most of this book describes what comprises the "people orientation" side of management. From good communication to passion, this 80% is something that a man or woman must possess because it can't be taught. A people orientation implies having a deep respect for others, no matter whether or not the others can help you along the way. An introvert can have the same love of people as an extrovert. A sullen personality still can have a heart of gold. The person who values people only as a means to an end can never succeed as a leader. Can this person rise to the top? Sure. Can he stay there? Not indefinitely.

Certainly, people have been known to change their belief systems. I have seen it happen, however, only to those who have experienced a life-altering moment of some type. Perhaps it was a heart attack or the loss of a spouse. For some, it was becoming involved in church. For others, it was marrying a soulmate who showed them a different path. So yes, people can change, but this 80% rule isn't an easy one to overcome if you don't have a people orientation today.

The "learned skills" that comprise 15% of a good leader are those skills that are needed to make them productive workers. A CFO needs to be an excellent accountant. A VP of marketing needs to understand positioning and advertising and public relations. Most people get a good start in college, and others learn on the job. However, true leaders never get to the point where they are satisfied with their level of knowledge. Learned skills become obsolete fairly quickly in today's world. The employees who don't embrace continued learning won't become leaders, and can guarantee that they will be passed by when it comes time to promote new managers. No one wants to work for somebody who knows less than or someone who is unwilling to try new technology.

The desire to learn is also an important indicator of passion. Leaders who have committed themselves to the company's product and philosophy naturally want to learn more ... about the customers, about the competitors, about technology, about scientific findings that relate to their field. It's a never-ending job to stay ahead of the marketplace and predict trends that can change the company.

Then there's the "gut." I have never met a good leader who doesn't have good instincts. I define "gut" as having the ability to assess the information at hand and make a decision that addresses the missing pieces that can't be analyzed. It involves taking what some people refer to as risks, but good leaders know there is much less risk than it appears.

"Gut" is why CEOs are paid so handsomely. And while this isn't a learned skill, some people can be taught to listen to their inner voice. They can become more effective at acting on their instincts. It takes experience, a few failures, a few more successes, and a nurturing boss or two before most people learn to trust their gut. It is an essential element of leadership. But can people without good instincts develop them? No, I don't believe they can.

• BOB McCURRY •

"John has not changed a bit.

He is the same man he was when we met on the

football field more than 50 years ago. He remembers

how he got where he is today, and knows that he

achieved this through people. He gives credit where

credit is due, through programs like profit-sharing.

It doesn't get much more basic than that."

THE WRONG KIND OF
ORGANIZATIONAL CHART

Obviously, it's a good idea to let people know who their supervisor is. I also advise telling people who heads their division and the name of the CEO. Unlike popular organizational management practices, I do not think all employees in the company need closely defined job descriptions, nor do they need titles that indicate their exact location in the company food chain.

Although many human resources experts have tried to convince me over the years that employees need a complete organizational chart, I never took their advice. As I discussed earlier, I believe it is so important to have the right people in the right place within an organization. When a chart is in place that shows progression from one position to the next, the hands of management are somewhat tied. Their ability to move people among departments or to handle different tasks within the same department is hindered when employees can claim that the staffing changes are not in line with the promises made on the organizational chart.

I have never wanted employees to view promotions or lateral job changes as unfair to other people at the same level. Without a strict organizational chart, we were more free to make the best employment decisions. It wasn't uncommon for employees to cheer for their peers when they were moved to a new position or put in charge of another department. Without a chart that told everyone where he or she was *supposed* to move, it was never a threat to see others succeed. All employees knew that perhaps it could be them next time. Without a chart, we could identify leaders and move them two rungs up the ladder in one day, and employees didn't have a chart to indicate they were supposed to be upset.

The wrong kind of organizational chart tends to instill a sense of entitlement. I see it in companies where I serve on the boards of directors. People who know their rank on the ladder begin to expect upward movement simply because it is their turn or because they have reached a milestone in their longevity with the company. Employees also tend not to look sideways at other opportunities within the company. I would rather have people who are as excited about lateral moves as they are about promotions. It was great to hear people in the company who truly felt that we put people in a position where their skills could be used most successfully. It was great to hear, "Wherever you need me, Mr. Mac."

The best reason for avoiding strict employee charts, graphs, and job descriptions is that they give people a reason *not* to be involved. By defining departmental boundaries and putting very specific responsibilities in writing, the message is clear: Do your job and your job only. All those who work in an atmosphere with strict job descriptions can tell they are surrounded by people who like to say or imply that "it's not my job." At Worthington Industries, our people knew that keeping the plant floor clean was everyone's responsibility, not just the job of the night janitors. Pride, not job descriptions, led our employees to be completely motivated to do the best work possible, and not to care if they would receive credit for it or not. So throw your charts and ladders out the window, and begin to build an environment in which all employees think they can rise to be in charge. Just ask Donal Malenick how he rose from a laborer to president of Worthington Industries. It's a story about a man who had more perseverance than anyone I have known and a great ability to get people to produce. I saw his potential, and he was willing to learn. Together, we expanded his career within the company that far exceeded what any organizational chart would have outlined for us.

MANAGEMENT BY MOVEMENT

A good man who never leaves his office cannot become a good leader. Without reaching out to visit employees and observing them working in their own element, there is no purpose to possessing any leadership skills. Just as a light loses its purpose if it is covered by a basket, a leader becomes irrelevant if contact with people is removed from the equation.

When Worthington Industries was in its early years, I spent time every day not just touring plants, but sometimes picking up tools and working in the plants. By doing this, I learned so much about the employees, the equipment, the clients, and the product. The plant visits not only allowed me to spread the message about my plans for the company, it also allowed me to develop innovative solutions to production problems and unusual client requests. The time I spent in the plants cannot be replaced, and I contend that it also was the most important reason why our company became the corporate giant it is today.

As time went on, it became harder for me to have the extended daily contact with front-line employees. The company grew quickly, and we opened multiple sites for our manufacturing processes. I was not able to visit the plants as often, but the employees understood, because by then we were very good at communicating our message from the top down. But don't think for a minute that I stopped spending time on the plant floor. Even today, I have a travel schedule that puts me in the plants several times a year. Because of our company's low turnover, I am able to see the people I know well on every trip. Eventually, I began using golf carts for my plant tours so that I could see more people in a shorter period of time.

The highlight for any leader who has taken the time to visit employees on their own turf is the look on people's faces when they have the opportunity to show off a new skill, a new product, or a new machine. To show me — the company founder who had many years working on the front line — something I don't know about technology would make employees so proud of the work they were doing. I wouldn't replace those visits for anything.

I always have a kind word for the employees I visit. This isn't a time to be the bearer of bad news or to find fault with systems or work habits. I let the supervisors handle those issues. Employees are glad to see me because I focus on recognizing their efforts, not their failures. Leaders who are feared or not respected aren't likely to be a motivating force when they visit employees. Attitude is everything when you're a boss who believes in making the rounds, as I do. Approach with a smile, share a juicy piece of information, and act as an *ear* not an *eye.* Trust that your supervisors are catching the infractions, and go out there with an interest in finding the good in people and hearing an idea or two that could revolutionize your business.

While CEOs can have a great impact on employees simply by

• DONAL MALENICK •

"Other CEOs from manufacturing companies were amazed at the harmony between plants and management. How does that happen? We made everyone feel like part of the team, and we proved that our management team was part of their team.

I'll never forget one day when the sales manager hit the roof after seeing a frivolous, unprofitable order come through the system. He called several people trying to find out who would take an order that would require so much manpower for so little reward. He soon found out that it was Mr. Mac, and was a little embarrassed for being so vocal about the order. But he still told Mr. Mac about it, just like he would have told any other sales rep.

The day we tooled up the machines to start that job, Mr. Mac came to the plant and worked on the order until it was shipped. The people who were there that day will never forget that Mr. Mac was part of their team, taking their lead. It has become one of the legendary stories of our company history."

walking around and staying on top of the organization's day-to-day operations, other levels of management must understand that walking around will have an impact on *themselves*. Those who take time to observe, listen, question, and communicate are the only worthwhile managers. One who is too comfortable with paperwork or expects people to come to him is not doing his job. Don't let him stay in that position, for he probably is making decisions without full knowledge of each situation. In addition, he probably is not communicating important information down the chain of command. Replace him with someone who wears walking shoes.

☞

EXPECT INPUT, DEMAND SUPPORT

I am a good listener. I can sit back and allow people to give me their reports and their recommendations. I ask questions and I expect answers — if not immediately, then within a day or two. I never have been afraid to ask for opinions, and I often keep an open mind until all the facts are in. But when I fully understand the situation and have had an opportunity to ruminate on those facts, I make a decision. Done.

No one is more detrimental to the efforts of a good leader than an employee who doesn't come on board with a decision after it has been

• JOHN P. McCONNELL •

"He appreciates every employee in this company,

and has put many things in place to prove his loyalty

to them. At one time, there were people who thought

he was crazy for doing all he did. Now, after seeing

our success, our level of productivity,

and our very low turnover, he's a genius."

made. The time for employees, and especially for VPs, managers, and supervisors to voice their concerns and take sides on an issue is during the analysis period. I often expected my upper-level management staff to be contrary while both sides of the issue were being weighed. Only by hearing the good, the bad, and the ugly can a leader be completely confident in the decisions he makes.

The problem typically comes after a decision has been announced and some factions of the organization vocally question the direction in which the CEO is heading. It's a disaster when a major decision is questioned. Morale becomes a problem, production can suffer, and the change that the CEO intended to make may never come to fruition. All supervisors must understand their role as part of the management team: to provide facts, share opinions, then march to the corporate drumbeat after a decision is made.

A strong corporate mindset, where managers are confident in the CEO's decisions, depends entirely on having someone at the helm who is a good, honest, fair, and ethical human being. Unless those characteristics are in place, neither the CEO nor the supervisor will be trusted and their decisions will be sabotaged. CEOs and managers who make poor decisions repeatedly will become less effective and will not reach the level of being considered a true "leader." I was never afraid to gather input.

• DONAL MALENICK •

"Mr. Mac always appreciated people speaking up,

as long as they did it before a decision was made.

Once a decision was on the table,

support was the only acceptable response."

My advisory staff always knew that my mind was not made up until everyone had their turn to speak. Because of that, my decisions were trusted. Even when they disagreed with my decisions, they knew the choice was not made in haste; and because they were part of the discussion, they understood the reasoning behind each decision and were able to communicate my intent without letting their own skepticism leech into the conversation.

Every business school student I have ever met understands that "decisiveness" is a necessary trait of good leadership. What isn't discussed enough in business schools is the responsibility every other leader in the organization has to internalize each decision and make it come to life.

☞

USE MEETINGS SPARINGLY

I've never been very patient with meetings. Some of the time they are necessary. Most of the time they simply take people away from their jobs. If you have a reason to meet, that's fine. Just stick to the task at hand. Know the purpose of your meeting before going into the room, and make sure all the employees are told in advance of the meeting why they have been invited and what is expected of them. Make sure that some, if not all, of the meeting participants come prepared with a report that will shine a light on the problem being discussed. Go around the room, hear reports, allow limited discussion, make assignments (if needed), then adjourn. In most of the meetings you lead, don't feel the need to make a decision in the room. It's good to gather information and decide later.

As a CEO or department leader, it can make sense to have a regular meeting with your top four or five officers. It's a good way to stay in touch. But don't expect these meetings to solve all the problems at hand. The agenda should be to hear reports from your officers ... and only from those who have a report to make. Think of your informational meetings as a football huddle. Only the people on the field for that play come together to quickly exchange ideas, hear a decision from the leader, then break to go do their work. Most corporate huddles last too long. Perhaps play clocks in the corporate world would be a good idea.

Think about the meetings you attend. Are you achieving anything by pulling so many high-paid people into one room? Keep in mind that meetings can be a stall tactic. They can be an excuse to look busy without taking action.

Your time is too valuable to spend it in meetings. Get out of your office or the conference room and solve problems where the rubber meets the road.

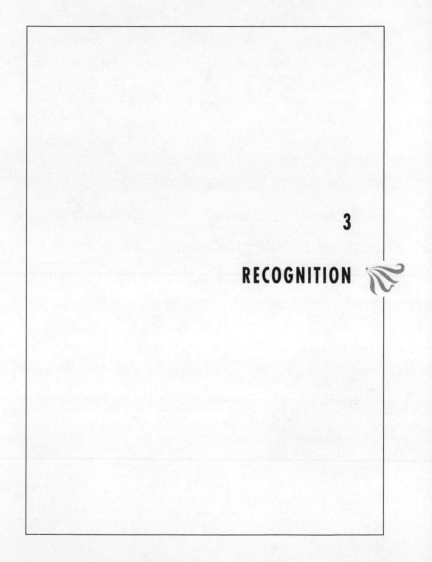

3

RECOGNITION

☞

PEOPLE ARE THE MOST IMPORTANT ASSET

Resources are important. I'm a big believer in capital resources that give employees the right tools and the right atmosphere to complete the job well. A solid brand name is an important asset, of course, as is a solid product. But the most important asset any company has is its people.

I warned readers at the beginning of this book that I will bring up "recognition" many times, and here it is again. Recognition, in this case, is a company's total and committed belief that nothing can be accomplished without the top performance of the people it employs. Nothing at all can be done well without people. Those who don't agree with me probably are having a hard time getting through this book. Everything I believe in, from management by walking around to the need for passion, comes from knowing that without my employees, Worthington Industries is nothing.

Think about the last planning meeting you attended, whether it was for your company, another business, your church, or a nonprofit organization. I'm sure all those who attended looked at the financial statements, and they probably heard a report on sales trends, investments, or marketing. But did anyone talk about the people? Did anyone suggest ways to improve the work environment or reward those who have been productive? Probably not. On a list of corporate resources, I would bet that fax machines and file cabinets are added to the list long before anyone thinks of including the employees.

Employees are not commodities that can be found in one homogenous labor pool. The group of people you have in place today is the key to your company's future, especially if you trust your hiring process and your front-line supervisors. Leaders must recognize that the best plans in the world will not be implemented successfully without a hard look and a long appreciation for the people charged with making it happen.

The next time you put together a planning agenda or make a list of your company's assets, don't forget to discuss the influences of employees. When a company begins to alter the way it views people, dramatic results can happen. Yes, I admit to enjoying the company of others. I appreciate people and have many lifelong friends. But there is a practical side to putting a high value on your employees: Happy employees produce — and they stay — and the company profits. Many of the programs we put in place to improve the lives of our employees have the added benefit of keeping them near their post. With a barbershop on site, no one is tardy returning to work after a haircut. Our medical center allows people to make short appointments during lunch breaks or immediately after work. So if you have a hard time believing that people should be treated well simply because they are human beings, then perhaps I have convinced you that there is an economical side to the issue, as well.

☞

IT IS ABOUT TEAM

It is hard to argue about the value of building a team among your employees. Put 10 people in a room doing separate chores, and they are soon tripping over each other with little to show for their efforts. On the other hand, put those same people in a room with the charge of working together, and the sum of the parts is more powerful than just the 10 individuals.

Good leaders understand the importance of teamwork. They are able to find opportunities for heads to come together to solve problems, and they understand that high-tech and labor-saving devices won't do the job; people working together toward a common goal will.

Many times, when our company faced problem projects or economic downturns, I watched our employees pull us through. We usually came out on top because the employees did not want to let each other

• JOHN P. McCONNELL •

"My father leads by doing. He has a humble style

that works well in this industry. He built many

different kinds of relationships because he likes to

interact with people. As a result of these relationships,

people did not know they were being led."

down. When necessary, they pitched in for each other. They gave a hand to crews that were short-staffed, and they worked together to find solutions. To a good team, seeing even one person affected by a layoff is a reflection on everyone, not just on management. A good team is just as likely to feel pain together as they are to celebrate together.

Building an atmosphere where teamwork can thrive takes work. Sometimes, it's like raising children: It's easier for supervisors to just do the work themselves than it is to go to all the trouble of delegation, problem-solving sessions, and group commitment. But in the end, one supervisor who continually saves the department will never be as effective as 50 men and women working on different shifts who are committed to making sure everyone has a job to come back to in the morning.

What does it take to build a good team environment? Belief in your people and recognition for their efforts are a good start. Leaders who don't trust the actions and decisions of others will unwittingly encourage individual activity and reward those who act outside the framework of the team. It may be good for the short-term, but lousy for the future.

When working to build a team-oriented company, it is important for supervisors to avoid creating programs, building incentives, or making decisions that reward only individuals and undermine the group

• DONAL MALENICK •

"There are a lot of things you can't teach people, such
as respect for others. Those who are deceitful and
self-serving never made it at Worthington Industries.
Those who didn't share credit for a job well done
never became part of our team. We wanted only
people who respected the man next to him,
the woman in the office, and the young boy on the
plant floor who just started last week."

comfort level. Friendly competition is important and can be motivating for many types of people, but if the rewards are too individually focused, the people whose personalities are naturally competitive may set themselves apart from the rest.

To build a team, all good leaders understand that, first and foremost, they must be the type whom others want to please. Good leaders motivate with a combination of high expectations and a high level of appreciation for work well done. When a team wants to accomplish a goal or beat a record, their main motivation is hearing a sincere "well done" from the top. Some CEOs have been written about because of their reputations as hard-nosed, driven men. Are they effective leaders? Perhaps in the short-term, but it can't last forever. Think back to the coaches you had as a child. Some were tough, yet they still were encouraging. Others were just plain mean — almost bullies. Remember how motivation by fear stopped working as soon as the coach left the room?

SHARE INFORMATION
— AND PROFITS

Most people have a hard time understanding the connection between their actions and the profitability of a company. If a line worker misses his mark again and again, the cost of the materials he is wasting doesn't necessarily concern him. A purchasing assistant who doesn't bid the cost of copy paper because it is only copy paper usually has no idea that she is taking a significant chunk of corporate profits. The connection between expenses and profits is not easily understood. On the other hand, employees do tend to understand that productivity and revenue are related. Whether we're talking about vice presidents or new laborers, the key is to make sure all those in the company relate their behavior and decisions to the success of the organization.

How can you make everyone, from the plant worker to the receptionist, understand their roles in profitability? Simple: You share the numbers. Do we open the books and expect our employees to peruse the complete financial statements? That wouldn't work. It's "too much information," as people say. Instead, we take time to craft the message in a way that is relevant. We have seminars with small groups of 20 to 30 people that are somewhat like mini-finance and economic lessons. In those meetings, we start by reviewing our current financial status then back it up with the sales outlook. What we find is that most people have great misconceptions about profit. Many people think if you sell a dollar's worth of product, you make a dollar. (National surveys show the average conception of corporate profits is 35% of sales.) To our employees, we might say, for example, "OK, you can't control the cost of the raw material, but you can control how much of it we use by reducing the scrap rate." We then show them in dollars and cents how much scrap was generated and what effect reducing that number would have on the bottom line. We do the same exercise with a number of the employee-controlled costs, such as absenteeism, rejection rates, equipment and supplies usage, and so on.

This type of communication is a constant thing. The classes are held on a regular basis to expose new employees to the profit-minded thinking we expect. We often end our sessions by showing how much more profit-sharing would be available with a lower scrap rate or better attendance. This really drives the point home, and people have no trouble relating to the numbers when we show how it impacts each of them personally.

In 1966, we told the employees we were going to change the incentive plan to bottom-line profit. We made sure that everyone understood that this new method would reward everyone fairly. The more money the company made, the more each employee would make, regardless of whether he or she was in production, maintenance, sales, or administration. We fixed the portion of pre-tax profit that would be paid out to employees at 16%. We tied the payout to salary so that employees would have incentive to try to improve their position in the company and take on more responsibility. The year that we introduced profit sharing, we did something else I was told would not work: All production employees were put on salary. We, in effect, elevated all plant people to the same level as those working in the office. Today, because of profit-sharing and the peer pressure it creates, our people police themselves. As a result, we have very few abuses of the salary plan. Our employees also are much more conscientious about costs and waste, which means that our quality also is very high. They care about what goes out the door.

I remember working as a laborer in the Oldsmobile division of General Motors, while I was a student at Michigan State University. No one at Oldsmobile cared what I thought about the company or my job. I had no personal connection to the profitability of the company and felt that the laborers around me were completely apathetic about the decisions being made in Detroit. Even then, the lack of motivation and productivity struck me as being a problem. I was able to reach production quota on any machine in the plant in less than five hours into an eight-hour shift, but my hands were slapped by the union. They said I needed to fill the full eight hours because the company's expectations were low and the union did not want them raised. Frankly, what did my co-workers care about how well General Motors was faring? It meant nothing to them. They still received a weekly paycheck.

When I started Worthington Industries, I was determined to do things differently; and I achieved that. Some years ago, *Forbes* magazine said this about us: "Everyone benefits equally at Worthington Industries, even the shareholders." I couldn't be more proud.

NO COFFEE BREAKS, BUT FREE COFFEE

For some reason, other CEOs are fascinated that even at the most entry-level positions, we do not have coffee breaks at Worthington Industries. We don't. Instead, we treat our employees like adults who are not necessarily better off when living on a predetermined eating schedule. It may work in kindergarten, but not in the "real world." We give our employees

• JOHN P. McCONNELL •

"For the most part, people like parameters, and they like to know when they have won or lost. If we can help define the finish line for them, they'll work to get there. As a result, the best way we communicate corporate expectations is through profit sharing."

all of the coffee they want at no cost, but we let them know that we will not shut down a machine just because it's 10:00 a.m. If 9:30 offers a better break in the work flow, go get yourself a cup. If you don't drink coffee or you're having a particularly productive day, thank you for staying at your machine to work. This is just one example of how we say to people, "You are a responsible person, and we trust your work ethic."

The health center we opened some years ago at the Worthington location is my pride and joy. It's another form of recognition that is appreciated by everyone in our company. I remember a time when we terminated 26 engineers because we had no jobs for them. I was particularly concerned about how one man would react. How did he? He sent us the kindest letter, thanking us for letting him be part of the team. In the letter, he mentioned the medical center and how appreciative he was that it was available to him and his wife when they needed it most.

Our people are our family. They enjoy the freedom we give them, as well as the extras. We benefit from their happiness with better productivity, lower turnover, and a long line of qualified applicants for every position we have open. Most of all, treating people this way is the right thing to do.

• DON MALENICK •

"He managed by setting an example. The most amazing thing is that Mr. Mac was this way from Day One. He never had to stop and plan his approach. Because he is so sincere in his ways, his influence continues to flow through the organization."

THE BOTTOM LINE: RESPECT

The first thing I do when we visit a plant we are considering for purchase is to look in their shower room and toilets. You'd be surprised at some of the working conditions I have seen. You wouldn't send a pig into some of these rooms. In 1973, we bought a plant in Chicago that had about 173 employees. They were unionized, but it was a very weak union. This particular plant had me a little worried about how their union would fit with our culture of freedom and movement and salaries. During my first visit, I walked into their locker room and the ceiling was sagging where their roof had leaked. The shower and toilets were filthy. The first thing I did when the purchase was finalized was to paint that locker room and make improvements to it. A year and a half later, the employees voted the union out. They realized what it meant to be respected, and they noticed that the union wasn't really working on their behalf.

We bought a plant in South Carolina with the same conditions. Another plant in Baltimore was the same story. I don't know how so many companies have gotten away with treating their employees like cattle, but it's still happening today. Respect for your people is something you feel deeply, and respect never can be proven by words alone. Action

TOM PETERS

excerpt from <u>Thriving on Chaos</u>

"Worthington Industries founder John McConnell

was considering buying a company awhile ago.

One of his acid, pre-acquisition tests is a tour of the

facilities. In the employee cafeteria, he found netting

temporarily rigged beneath the ceiling ... to catch the

crumbling plaster and keep it out of the food.

It led him to question the whole deal.

If management was that insensitive to its

work force, could the company be salvageable?"

must accompany it. We had three or four guys who were from Mexico working in a plant we purchased in Chicago. They couldn't speak English, so we helped them learn. Now they are three of our best employees.

I always expected our personnel departments to know everyone in the plants. In the mid-1960s, we had a few excellent employees who weren't learning as quickly as others. The personnel man recognized their talent, talked to them a bit about it, and discovered that they couldn't read. Instead of firing them or wondering how to replace them, we sent them to school to help them learn.

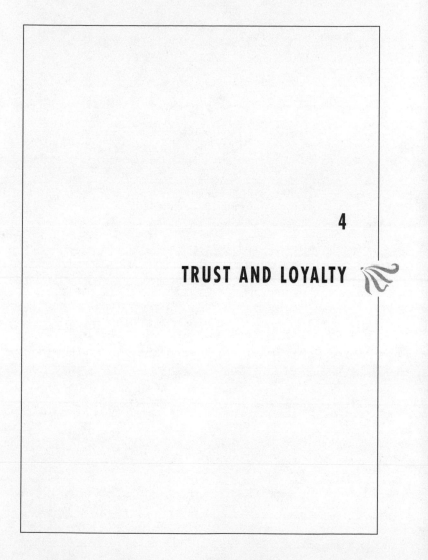

4

TRUST AND LOYALTY

☞

'NO' TO UNIONS

Arguments used to start whenever I would mention my disdain for labor unions. Part of me doesn't like the fact that unions were forced to form, and I'm embarrassed that companies treated their employees so poorly. The rest of me does not like the adversarial relationship that unions have created between employees and corporate leaders. What a shame it had to happen. How much more could be accomplished if Americans had spent the last century working together — the hands that build the products, the managers who make things hum, and the capital influx that the leadership represents. It's sad, really.

At one time, unions were an important way for workers to organize for fair treatment and safe working conditions from companies that had no respect for them. But somewhere along the way, unions went awry. Their demands and expectations began to be unreasonable, and their presupposition that management was always against the employees was harmful and counterproductive. I am convinced that only harm comes from having a strong union in place. When there are unions, trust and loyalty are a casualty. I have experienced it first hand, even from a laborer's point of view. Union bosses have a way of taking the most well-intentioned young man and turning him into a skeptic who believes that he is being used. Not many people will be productive when they think only management benefits from their work and they themselves will suffer. Nor will employees be interested in productivity, efficiency, and eliminating waste if they are taught to distrust the goal of profitability. To union workers, everything they touch is management money, which makes it dirty money. Nothing positive comes from a relationship like this.

I do recognize, however, that some companies deserve a critical appraisal from their employees. I have seen those companies in action. As a matter of fact, I have chosen not to purchase several companies that had built an employee base that held such animosity that nothing I could do would repair it. My message to corporate leaders is this: If you don't provide your employees with a safe environment and give them the recognition they deserve for their hard work, you deserve criticism. If you don't tell employees what you expect and give clear direction for their work, you deserve to have people who are aimless in their work ethic. But unions have no place in a company where the operations are clearly defined, where equipment is maintained, where leadership is fair, honest, and straightforward, where pay and benefits are market value or better, and where employees are informed. To CEOs, I say, do these things, and your employees will not want to be represented by an outside party. Even the most liberal employees today recognize that unions are not for them. People who have joined our company share their experiences of working in a union shop and tell how they felt used as objects for negotiations and pawns in an ongoing chess game with management. They didn't like it. For them, the Worthington Way is much better.

The productive, nonunion shop is not a fairy tale. I can cite several cases in which unions were forced out by the workers when we proved that our intentions were good. Worthington Industries purchased two companies — one in Chicago and one in Baltimore — where unions were decertified because the people believed in our management over their own. It's important to note that we didn't just get lucky; we proved ourselves to them. We showed them how we would clean up their workspace, provide them with the right machinery to do their jobs well, give them supervisors who would treat them with respect, and allow them to share in the profits of the company. They were impressed that we would do all of this without forcing months of negotiations and risk having their benefits cut … which is what a union would do for them.

From the beginning, when I founded Worthington Steel, I wanted to reward employees for their hard work. I always saw employees as my partners. If they succeeded, I succeeded. If they came up with better ideas, we all benefited. I made sure of that. Then, in 1966, when I put a

• TOM PETERS •

excerpt from <u>Thriving on Chaos</u>

"It is commonly assumed that the high wages

of unionized steelworkers doomed integrated steel

manufacturing in this country.

The high pay at Nucor, Chaparral and

Worthington Steel makes a mockery of this."

formal profit-sharing plan in place, the industry roared. "Why," people asked, "would you want to give your hard-earned money to "them?" I reminded the skeptics that the "hard-earned" part was the role of the laborers. Our plan worked. Now it's hard to find a company that doesn't do it.

Never have I regretted the decision to share profits. And never have I doubted the wisdom of it. But our system of sharing the rewards doesn't sit well with unions. They don't want to be tied that closely to management, and they don't want their union members to help the company other than by showing up every day and performing the minimum that is expected of them.

Other than their hostility toward management, I have another major problem with unions: They expect members to show allegiance always to the union and never to the company. Individuals are not allowed to state opinions that are not in line with the union bosses. Workers who happen to agree with management on a contentious issue are shut down quickly. Their opinions don't matter, and they may be denied promotions or raises. To unions, the success of the company is not relevant, as long as their people are being paid. The power of the union bosses is far-reaching, and management is not allowed to gain favor among the membership. How can anyone think unions are a good idea? Labor and

management must work as a team or we will not survive as a company ...
or a nation.

☞

INCENTIVES CAN'T WORK
WITHOUT TRUST

It has always been important to me to have a strong incentive program.
Not only is compensation important, but "comp time" and extra rewards
matter, too. I have seen employees respond amazingly well when they see
a direct connection between their efforts and their pocketbooks. But sometimes that connection is broken. The thread that ties management and
their employees is a fragile one, and it's based on trust. Destroy that trust,
and the advantage of any incentive program is lost.

I have had many conversations with CEOs who have claimed they
see no correlation between their incentive programs and productivity.
Often, I find out that their management team does very little to share
information with employees. They write an annual check or plop a sum
of money into a retirement account for the employees without ever telling them how it gets there. Management must build a connection between
the work of the employees and their incentive pay. When a company

conveys its financial status, teaches employees about the impact of waste on profitability, and demonstrates the impact that absenteeism has on profits, then employees will understand. If a company even thinks about fudging the numbers it gives employees, management must understand that they are setting in motion a destructive force. Why would an employee work hard for the good of the company after learning that the CFO has been less than honest in the profitability reports? What incentive remains for employees who discover that management defines "profitability" using the formula that best suits them? Shame on you, if you have done any of these things.

Management has a lot of power in an incentive-driven organization. Abuse that power and employees may stay, but they certainly won't be cheering for the "bad guys" anymore. As a matter of fact, they may become a party to the downfall of the company.

At the top, leadership must set the standards for honest relationships at all levels of the company. By living ethical lives, treating the management team with honesty and fairness, and showing the utmost respect for employees, trust will permeate the company. But it's fragile. Good leaders protect this relationship with their lives.

Trust is a two-way street. I don't mean to imply at all that only management has a role in keeping the relationship solid. In many ways

• JOHN P. McCONNELL •

"My father is not an 'in-your-face' leader, and is very perceptive about human nature. He believes that too many rules communicate to employees that 'we don't trust you.' Most of all, he has such a deep respect for people that he wants to share his success with them."

over the years, I made it clear that I expected loyalty from employees, just as I would give loyalty to them. For example, laborers at Worthington Industries are salaried employees. They are paid even if they stay home sick. But I made it clear that if people called in sick to spend the day fishing, it was viewed as a breach of loyalty.

Another example of setting expectations of employees is how we measured workflow and productivity. All supervisors set productivity goals for their factory workers and made such a big deal about meeting or exceeding those goals that employees knew their loyalty to the company was shown by how hard they worked. Many of our supervisors and plant managers are good about using quotas to create a little competitive spirit. It's fun for people whose jobs can be mundane to work together to break the production number set by the shift crew before them. I remember that exhilarating feeling myself of creeping near a record-breaker on a particular machine. It's called "instant gratification," and we all enjoy it. One of my grandsons worked in the plant and called me several times to tell me how proud he was that his crew was breaking their *own* records. I love to see people possess that kind of spirit for their work.

As old-fashioned as it sounds, this is still a favorite saying of mine: "An honest day's pay for an honest day's work."

☞

TRUST EMPLOYEES
TO KNOW WHAT'S NEEDED

Trust can do many things for a company. Happy, productive workers are one outcome. Profitability is another. Part of that trust is believing that employees will know what's best for them. I always believed in giving my input, then getting out of the way.

Micromanaging is harmful. It tells employees you don't trust their actions or their decisions. Any company leader that jumps over a supervisor to give direction to an underling is micromanaging. Certainly, it's important for leaders to have contact with employees at all levels. But the gist of that contact is what matters. If a supervisor and his crew feel strongly that a new piece of equipment will be better for the company, and they have gone through the proper channels to purchase it, don't question the decision. Instead, visit the employees after the machine is up and running to see it for yourself and ask them to give you a demonstration. Thank them for watching out for the best interests of the company, and let them know you're looking forward to seeing the results of their decision. With that kind of trust, they won't disappoint you.

I have known CEOs who want approval on every purchase from

$500 and up. Half the time, they say "no" to requests, even if employees prove their case. Why do they do that? I think it's just to show who is the boss. Baloney! If you have the right employees with the right supervisors, and the trust runs deep between all parties, let employees make decisions that improve their environment and their productivity.

☞

ADMIT MISTAKES

Admit when you are wrong. Period. There is no better way to demonstrate your honesty and to earn respect from employees.

I must admit that the first couple of times I had to face employees and tell them, "I messed up," it was very hard. I tossed and turned at night, and spent hours practicing how I would break the news. After a while, admitting errors in judgment became easier, and the results of my confessions rose beyond my expectations. Every time I went to employees to tell them what I had missed or what decisions had gone wrong, I also told them how I planned to rectify the situation. Everyone is drawn to humble leaders. However, those who have humility yet don't provide bold solutions will be viewed as weak. It's important, after the confession, to show employees that you still are in control of the situation.

Therefore, prepare your case well and develop the resolution for the problem before making your wrongdoings public.

CEOs who don't admit mistakes can cost their company dearly. History if full of businesses that should have cut their losses by discontinuing a product or closing down a division. Most of the time, those hard decisions are not made because the leadership is not able or willing to say, "I was wrong." Over the years, I developed some great products that never sold. For instance, I had a patent for a safety clutch on lawnmowers, but the lawnmower companies didn't want it. To overcome their apathy, we tried to make lawnmowers ourselves. About four years after we started our lawnmower manufacturing line, we shut it down, realizing we were not in the consumer products business — nor should we be.

Another example was the time I built an entire plant for a coated-glass product. We thought we had the best technology in the business, but we didn't. The supplier who told us that sold us a bill of goods. Our product was marginally successful, but would not have been profitable for us over the long haul. I saw our mistake, admitted it to myself and to others, and got out of the business.

I'm convinced there were employees who knew that neither lawnmower manufacturing nor coated-glass production were in our best interests, but when the CEO said, "Go," they had no choice but to help make it happen. Who knows how much the company would have been affected and our profitability diminished if I had not admitted to the error of those two decisions. How much capital would have been pumped into those divisions before the company went broke?

Think about the times in your life when you have lost trust in friends and leaders. Almost always, it comes after an episode of hidden mistakes. Before creating a culture where admitting mistakes is a virtue, leaders must first feel comfortable communicating that mistakes are not a problem for anyone. Punishing those who don't own up to a mistake is understandable. Punishing those who make a well-intentioned error is unforgivable. Mistakes often are an indication that a risk was taken. And risks are the only way to make a leap in growth.

I remember watching Don Malenick start to blossom, long before he began moving up the chain of command to become Worthington Industries' president. He had a knack for leadership and great native intelligence. Don had a way of getting right to the problem and searching for an effective solution. But the most important trait I saw in him — the trait that led me to groom him as president — was that Don never gave an excuse as to why something wasn't done. His word was golden. If he said he would do it, he would do it. If he goofed, he came to me before

• DONAL MALENICK •

"Mr. Mac pushed responsibility and authority down to the lowest level. He always wanted people making their own decisions, even if they were bad decisions. We all quickly learned that mistakes were acceptable, as long as we admitted them and made them with the company in mind, not our own self interests."

anyone else could tell me about it. And he always had a solution for repairing the damage done. A great man.

☞

TRUST AND LOYALTY APPLY TO CUSTOMERS AND VENDORS

It follows that if you expect a motivated, unassuming work force, you also need customers who hold the same values. Over the years, we have gladly discontinued relationships with customers and vendors who were less than honest. Companies that consistently tried to pin their mistakes on our people, or vendors that always had an excuse for why their delivery dates weren't met didn't mesh well with Worthington Industries. Employees became frustrated when they repeatedly took the blame for things they were not responsible for doing. If we had not divorced these clients or vendors, employees would quickly get the message that management values profitability over honest working relationships.

When you read "Our Philosophy," it is evident that we are a customer-oriented company. Even before it was fashionable, I was talking about the importance of satisfied customers. For those who trusted us enough to send the primary portion of their business our way, we would

• TOM PETERS •

excerpt from <u>Thriving on Chaos</u>

"I've never visited a Worthington facility when

customers weren't present ... not just touring,

but working. Managers in Worthington factories are

routinely expected to spend about 15 percent

of their time on the road with customers."

respond accordingly. Ask our employees, and they also will tell you that without loyal customers we have nothing. More than just a supplier, Worthington Industries has always communicated to customers that "we're here for handling your hardships." Difficult decisions, difficult predicaments, and difficult specifications do not scare us. They energize us.

As with employees, I believe that customer relationships are a two-way street. We're honest with them about missed deadlines or overpromises we have made, and we expect them to be honest about everything from deadlines to cost expectations. Mutual respect is the key to long-term partnerships.

In the same way that we care about our customers, I have always valued relationships with vendors. When you build a relationship based on timely payment of invoices, honesty when problems arise, and realistic expectations, the benefits of that relationship are great. Many, many times, our loyal vendors have pulled us out of rough spots by going above and beyond the call of duty. We know they wouldn't do these favors for just any customer, only for those they trust and appreciate.

☞

LEARN TO SAY 'I DON'T KNOW'

Back to my friend and confidante Don Malenick. One thing I always remember about his leadership style is that Don was not afraid to say "I don't know." He never made up an answer or blamed someone else for not keeping him informed. And I had the chance to see that trait in him often, for I prided myself in asking good questions — questions that would get to the heart of the matter. Often, I intended the questions to be thought-provoking and didn't expect the person to have the answer at the tip of their tongue. I guess you could say I tested people and judged their integrity from the way they responded.

Like Don, the best leaders are those who can say "I don't know." But there's more. The best leaders also say "I'll find the answer." The people I admire are those who understand that the higher they climb, the less they know. The effort it takes to uncover an answer to a problem leads to personal and professional growth.

I never had to remind Don of the answers he had volunteered to find. He always came back to me in a short amount of time. And when he returned, he not only had an answer but also an idea on how he could put the answer to good use. He recognized that information is power, and the more information he sought, the better leader, steel man, and person he would become.

If you're looking for answers on what it takes to build or identify good character, the phrase "I don't know" is probably an important one to add to your vocabulary.

☞

AMERICAN WORK ETHIC: ALIVE AND WELL

Turn on the news any given night and you'll hear someone mourning the loss of the American work ethic. Reporters and business owners all seem to think that the human characteristic of wanting to work hard — and be appreciated for it — no longer exists. For anyone who thinks that, I challenge you. Here's the contest: Give me employees who seem unmotivated or difficult to deal with, and I'll find a way to bring out the best in them. By showing appreciation to an unmotivated worker, I have seen them produce like never before in hopes of being noticed again. I have watched difficult employees rise to the top of the list in productivity after they are assigned to posts where very little personal interaction is needed. Bosses who don't recognize their people are lacking a strong work ethic.

I have seen thousands of employees move through the company in the past 50 years. All of them, with few exceptions, responded with enthusiasm and rewarded me with higher productivity when they saw how fairly they would be treated and how often their efforts would be recognized. It's human nature to want to do well and to be thanked for a job well done. Don't discount today's workers because of a few bad eggs. And don't blame employees for the poor job you have done in motivating them.

Whatever the method of motivation, you must make employees feel they are part of a team and be willing to reward them for their efforts. I was born and raised with the Protestant work ethic that said everybody wanted to get ahead, everybody was willing to go to work, and everyone wanted to do a good job. Yes, the work ethic has changed a bit. Perhaps different things motivate people today. However, corporate management has not changed enough to appreciate the new work ethic. Some CEOs still manage the same way they did 30 years ago. They sit by the time clocks and bark at those who punch in late. They spend their day finding fault with people, and they're glad when they identify someone who should be fired. This "method" of motivation doesn't work. We have to innovate and try new concepts because people want to work. I believe that. It's up to you to figure out what motivates your people.

KEEP AN EYE ON EXECUTIVE COMPENSATION

Don't boards of directors understand the difference between company owners and paid executives? One has built an organization, created a base of employment, and contributed to the GNP. The other is an professional manager — an employee. One takes risks and puts his money and reputation on the line. The other pays for trial and error by using other people's money. One deserves compensation for all he has built. The other deserves compensation based on his contribution to the company at the time he is there.

Professional managers are a relatively new phenomenon in this country, and I don't like how loosely they are rewarded. No one is worth a million dollar base salary.

I am often amazed when I hear how much CEOs and CFOs and COOs make in today's corporations. Who has made the judgment that their contribution to a company is so much higher than the man who supervises a plant full of people working 24-hour shifts?

Incentives and bonuses that are based on measurable contributions to a corporation are fine. It's good to put a carrot in front of executives who are motivated by money. However, a pay level that is too high results in a system that rewards failures as well as successes. It creates a front office full of people who know they'll be able to afford fine dinners and country club fees no matter how their decisions impact the bottom line. Executive salaries have gotten out of hand. Period.

Until fifty years ago or so, entrepreneurship had its reward. Those who established a business and put their own sweat, tears, and money into building the company could be handsomely paid. Today, all it takes for some executives to become wealthy is an MBA and a few buddies on a board of directors.

I remember some years ago when I visited a group of men who were working late into the night to complete a plant expansion. It was very cold that night, so just before I left I had them promise they would go home, too. Out of respect to me, they said they would leave. I learned the next day that no one went home until the job was finished — many hours later. Because of their hard work, the plant opened sooner than expected, and we were able to create revenue ahead of schedule. What those men accomplished in one night directly affected our bottom line. Yet, in today's corporations, executives in the front office are taking home a salary that is 10 to 20 times greater than the wages of employees who make a difference every day on the plant floor.

5

IT'S ABOUT CHARACTER

Everyone agrees that good leaders have good character. Honesty, fairness, and a sense of self are vital for anyone who manages an entire company or a department of five. It's as important for the man on the line as it is for the man in the corner office. Where can character be found? Everywhere.

☞

HOCKEY PLAYERS AS EXAMPLES

When I hired our first manager of the Columbus Blue Jackets, a new NHL team, I was looking for a man of experience, humility, and character. I found that in Doug MacLean. When I first met Doug and told him how much I liked his leadership skills, he responded with uncertainty, not arrogance. "I know hockey, but do I know how to build a franchise from scratch?" he asked. I had seen enough of his confidence and common sense to know that he had what it takes. I convinced him of that, as well, and he has proven us both right.

Not only did I want to build a team that had a man of great character at the top, I also wanted to build a team of good men on the ice. Doug shared my desire to do so. Today, I am very proud of the Blue Jackets team — not only of their talent, but also of their charac-

• DOUG MACLEAN •

"Mr. Mac took immediately to the sport of
hockey because he thought the players were
such good guys. The first NHL draft we attended,
he was impressed with how many of the players
went immediately to hug their parents after their
name was called in the draft. It touched him.

Now Mr. Mac rarely misses a game.
The Blue Jackets have become a big part of his life."

ter. I have come to enjoy hockey immensely and have learned a lot about what hockey players are made of.

Many of the professional hockey players today are from humble backgrounds ... from families with hard-working parents dedicated to making their own way in the world and raising children of quality. To become good enough to play in the NHL requires a commitment from the kids and their parents to make the long, frequent drives to and from games and to show up for hours and hours of practice every week. In most parts of the world today, hockey is nearly a year-round sport for children, as well as for the pros.

Because of the nature of the game, most hockey players are pretty tough cookies. They are always ready to battle on the ice, and often carry the same intensity to other areas of their lives. They are spirited, quick, and willing to change. Most Importantly, they know the meaning of "team." Few hockey games are won by hotshots. It usually takes everyone on the ice to pull a victory out of the battle. Although they are tough, hockey players also have a good sense of right and wrong. Their families instilled this in them. And even though these men seem so rough on the ice, meet them in person and you'll realize they are very polite, appreciative people.

Although the NHL has been in existence since the early 1900s, the sport still is in its infancy as far as building a fan base. Hockey fans, in general, are very loyal to the sport. If they can afford it, they buy season tickets, even though more than 35 or 40 home games are on the schedule every year. What hasn't happened yet to hockey players is that their stars have not been elevated to the level of "American heroes" like the stars of the NFL, NBA, or MLB have. These hockey players realize they need their fans, and not the other way around. They are accessible to their fans. They don't have the same ultra-egos that are seen in other major league sports. That's good for the fans, and for the owners.

I have met other professional athletes, and I can say, unequivocally, that hockey players have the best set of values. The Blue Jackets players and I view life alike, because we all come from the same working-class, blue-collar backgrounds.

What do I appreciate most about hockey? It's a game of passion. No one can succeed on the ice unless he wants to win more than anything. If a player doesn't have passion on any given night, it's easy to spot. The coaches know it, the fans know it, I know it, and their teammates know it. Passion is what moves the puck down the ice. It's what keeps the other team's puck out of the goal. Corporate leaders can learn a lot from the desire of hockey players: They understand the goal, they know they have limited time to achieve it, they don't "hotdog" it, and they understand that mental preparation can make the difference between having an on or off night. Most of all, they have fun. They love the game of hockey and do their best when they play.

One season, we were having a particularly rough time, with quite a few consecutive losses. I approached the team in the locker room before the game and said, "I still love you, and the people still love you, so relax. Go out there and pretend that you're still 16 years old and you're getting ready to play hockey on the farm pond. Tonight, go out there and have that much fun again." I think they won that game 6–2.

☞

THE BIGGEST FLAW OF ALL

Good character is easy to define. The problem is that it's not always easy to identify. I have hired people who said the right thing, and even spent months or years *doing* the right thing, then came to a point when they made a move that lacked character.

What is the biggest flaw of all? It's the horrible distinction of being a self-serving human being. This is a dangerous type of person to employ. I've worked with a few, although not many. There's no telling how a self-serving person will impact the company. If every move and

• DONAL MALENICK •

"Building the Columbus Blue Jackets gave

Mr. Mac a new look on life. Yes, he's having

a lot of fun with this team, but it's important for

everyone to know that he's not doing it for himself;

he's doing it for the city of Columbus."

every decision is made by someone who is "doing what's best for me," then every move and every decision is tainted. Employees who are more concerned about their rise up the ladder, about the perks they can get from vendors, or about who they can rub shoulders with are going to be faced with moments when they must choose what is *not* best for the company.

Self-serving employees at the lower levels are bad enough, but self-serving leaders are far worse. I have known people who think they have inherent rights because of their position in a company. They see every decision as an opportunity to profit in some way. There is no doubt that these leaders will take many others with them down a twisted path. Although self-serving leaders have built financially strong companies, they can't build great companies. There comes a time when they self-destruct.

Every day that I went to the office, I looked out the window and considered all the decisions I had to make to keep those plants operating. I spent time contemplating how to make the processes better, our customer service more responsive, our clients more loyal. Never did it cross my mind that I had to make myself richer or my domain larger. I made every decision for *them* — my employees and customers.

I remember one newly hired supervisor who was given his new office and didn't seem happy with what he had. Over the weekend, he moved furniture into his office that we had set aside for another department. Nobody said a word to him, but the following weekend, others in the company moved everything back. He didn't last long.

Self-serving individuals are dangerous to a culture. They chip away at trust, and they raise questions about the people who hired them. If an employee or manager is concerned about how he can benefit, then every decision is viewed with a jaundiced eye. It impacts productivity *and* the bottom line. Don't allow it. Any leaders who think they may have this fatal flaw should take time to assess their character and find a way to make drastic changes. Only companies with leaders who believe the corporation has a bigger purpose than they do will succeed in business, and in life.

Character is not something you can take off and put back on when needed. Anyone who thinks you can live a personal life of lies and bad relationships while being an exemplary leader is wrong. And you can bet that the CEO who spends his time at the office scheming is not someone I would want to invite for dinner.

A TEAM SPORT ADVANTAGE

Character comes from many sources. For most people, their family life determines how they will view the world. However, I believe that many events in our lives can be character building. Tragedies, for example, can force people to find a reservoir of empathy and grace inside themselves. I believe that involvement in team sports is another important teacher when it comes to learning the value of good character.

A business analyst asked me one time why we had so many football players on our staff. I responded with many reasons why I find the experience of playing football a valuable one. First and foremost, football players understand that no one can succeed without a great team. When men play football, the concept of "team" isn't just a lesson on the chalkboard or in a textbook.

Another reason I see value in football players is that they understand that getting knocked down is part of the game. The difference is whether or not you get back up and how long it takes to do that. "Shake it off" is common advice I hear my football-player managers say to their employees. They don't let the occasional fumble mar the progress of the team. To them, a win never seems out of the question. They understand

• MICK McDANIEL •

"You are more likely to find people like John coming from small towns because they don't have to hustle to get ahead. They don't have to step on bodies. John understands poor and has empathy for those on both sides of the track. He never pushed anyone around, and most of his thinking is guided by the Golden Rule."

that you don't quit; that a game is never won or lost until the final buzzer.

We have built a company to complement the personality of the people we hire. We always liked to employ people who enjoy their work, so we created an atmosphere where competition was part of our workday. Contrary to what some people think, a competitive spirit helps build teamwork and grow relationships. It doesn't divide; it makes work fun.

I'm a steel salesman. I'm used to people telling me to get lost. However, that isn't what I hear. I hear opportunities. Instead of hearing, "We're not interested," I hear, "We're not interested in that particular product at this particular time and this particular price." To me, the door is open for a future relationship. The buzzer didn't end the game yet. *That* is what team sports have taught me.

MISTAKES ARE OK

I've never been afraid of mistakes, and I have made my share. I am confident in my ability to ask the right questions, seek advice from top counselors, weigh the factors, and listen to my gut. If the decision I make doesn't work the way I planned, then it's just another lesson learned. I chalk it up as another item on my valuable list of What Not To Do.

Because I believe strongly that mistakes are just inches away from being great ideas, I also have a high tolerance for mistakes among my managers and supervisors. The outcome of a decision isn't as important to me as the intent. Those who make a decision with the company's best interest in mind are doing the right thing, as far as I'm concerned. Certainly, I want to know that the employee who made the mistake based his or her decision on enough evidence, but that is not usually the problem.

I know people who lose many nights' sleep when they make a decision that doesn't pan out. They wonder what they did wrong and what they could have done differently. While that assessment is not a bad exercise to go through, the danger comes when leaders are paralyzed to make other decisions for fear that they will be wrong. I never have been one to second-guess myself. I trust myself enough to know that I used the best information I had available and made the best decision I could at the time. The result of this philosophy is a group of managers and a work force that actually is encouraged by how I handle mistakes. They see opportunity for themselves to make decisions without fear of repercussion. I have had many people over the years tell me how much they appreciated being allowed to fail. It has made them better employees, and better people.

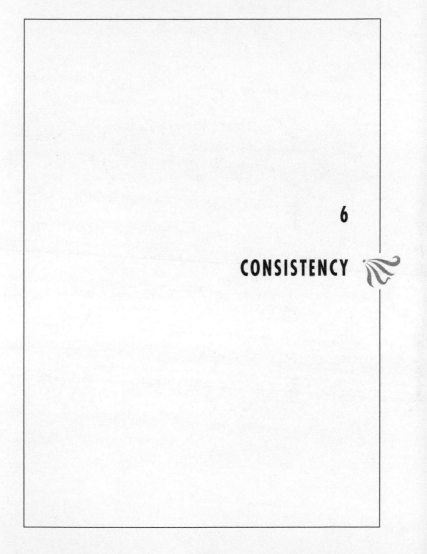

6

CONSISTENCY

I DON'T WORRY

Perhaps it's because I have been down most paths before, but I just don't worry. I don't remember a time when I stayed up at night thinking about my work. I have yet to lose sleep in the nights that come before speaking to my board, even if the news wasn't good. Perhaps my lack of worry is a virtue of living a long life. I have experienced so much in my 80-some years, and have been amazed many times at how much good can come out of adversity. I'm not afraid of what's around the corner.

I have always worked, it seems. I don't remember a life without a paycheck and a boss. When I was 10 years old, I hoed corn for 10 cents an hour. I don't remember thinking it was hard work, or feeling sorry for myself for giving up playtime to work in a cornfield. It was my situation, and I lived with it. From that early age, I observed supervisors and mentors who put their heart into their work and went full steam ahead into the next set of tasks they had to accomplish. Even in those days, I remember noticing how problems in life had a way of being resolved. It didn't matter whether we spent a lick of time worrying about it; problems happened and problems went away. To me, the time spent worrying was time that could have been used for more useful ruminations.

Many people have told me over the years how calming it is to be with someone who doesn't worry. I understand that. Whether it's been a friend, one of my managers, or a laborer in the plant, even I find myself energized by people who don't pine for "what could be" but instead look for ways to improve their situation. Leaders who spend time thinking and talking about actions that will move the business forward are much more likely to have people get on board with them than those who are looking for whom or what to blame.

Worry is an indication of uncertainty. It shows lack of vision and lack of confidence. Leaders who have a tendency to fret over issues often don't see the impact that their anxiety has on the people around them. Their employees look to their leaders to be the ones who are not affected by adversity, but instead are the ones who see beyond today's troubles to develop solutions for tomorrow. Perhaps the most dangerous impact of apprehension is that it is contagious. And if it spreads, it can paralyze a company.

A good leader believes in himself. He knows what to do when he gets knocked down and exudes an air of quiet confidence. Leaders who are not at that point in their professional lives should take a quick assessment of the times when they have failed. Think hard about how the situation turned out, and believe in your abilities to make the right decision in the face of adversity. Know that you will survive, no matter how much agonizing you do.

Employees want to know that their leaders are in control — of the company, and of their emotions. An inconsistent leader cannot be a good leader, for once employees feel that the person at the wheel is wavering and worrying, the chain of trust is broken. Those who spend time in a state of anxiety are not stable, reliable sources of decision making. By worrying, rather than acting upon a situation, the message is sent that the company's future is uncertain.

ASK FOR INPUT, THEN GO

Consistent leaders are those who have their thumbprint on every major decision the company makes. Whether you founded your company or were hired to run it, you are in charge for a reason. People at all levels look to you for wisdom and discernment. Not only should you want to *know* about the major issues facing your company, you should want to be *involved* in them. People expect you to be involved. Allowing others to determine the direction of the company is shirking your duty. It's irresponsible and detrimental. You, alone, are the keeper of the vision.

In the early years, I knew each man and woman who worked for me. For many years, I saw every employee every day. Back then, it was easy to communicate my wishes, and they heard every decision from me. If a decision seemed odd or out of character, they would simply ask me about it. Consistency was easy because I was the one delivering the ideas and communicating the direction. Obviously, size changed all of that. We reached a point where only a few people would hear decisions right from my mouth, and then were charged with carrying out the order. Even with these layers of people, my message came through clearly. I always knew where the company was headed, and I made decisions consistent with that direction and with our philosophy. Because of that certainty, even shift employees whom I didn't see on a regular basis *knew*, by the spirit of each decision, that it came from me. That's what consistency in leadership is all about.

Consistency in both direction and decision is key. The only way to have consistency is to be decisive. As Worthington Industries grew, I quickly saw how little time I had to spend on every decision that arose because new issues seemed to crop up by the minute. Of course, I began to rely on others to do the research and develop a recommended course of action. I always believed in hiring good people around me; therefore, I always listened intently to their wise counsel. Sometimes, their recommendations were right on target; other times, I found myself coming up with alternate solutions and asking others for feedback. But in the end, I always trusted my gut to make the decision. It was my thumbprint that sealed the deal. People at all levels knew that Mr. Mac was in charge, and they trusted me to decide what was best for the company.

Good leaders don't worry about gaining support from 100% of the people *before* a decision is made. That kind of thinking only leads to long, drawn-out, watered down decisions. What good leaders should expect is consensus *after* a decision is made. As long as my managers believed that I studied the information and solutions they provided, they felt good about the end result. They believed in me and in the fact that I put the company first and included the Golden Rule as part of every decision.

☞

YES, CONSISTENCY
CAN INSPIRE INNOVATION

As I said earlier, the philosophy of Worthington Industries was set the day I founded the company. The "Our Philosophy" card that every employee owns was written more than 30 years ago and remains unchanged. There is not a person in the company today who doesn't know the prin-

• MICK McDANIEL •

"John doesn't do things half-cocked.

He takes time to make decisions, but his

top priority in every decision is

to do the right thing."

ciples of our daily operation: We open the door each day to earn money for shareholders, to honor and recognize our employees, to serve our customers, to respect our suppliers, and to expect a hard day's work from everyone involved with Worthington Industries.

Sounds cozy, doesn't it? It is my sincere belief that consistency creates a garden from which ideas grow. It's not necessary to write a sexy new message in every newsletter we publish. When people understand the company's purpose well, they are free to develop any ideas that fit that purpose. What keeps people in a state of inactivity are the CEOs who change course as often as they change shirts. Leaders who are not consistent in their messages or their beliefs create a pool of people who never quite understand the company's direction well enough to improve processes, change the way customers are serviced, or develop new products. Consistency is crucial.

I can remember many discussions where plant supervisors would say to me, "Since we believe in such-and-such, can I suggest a better way to make that happen?" In other words, the spirit of our company philosophy was so strong that employees at all levels internalized it and helped move every facet of our production and service in line with it.

People often ask me whether or not my style is transferable to any other industry. Yes, of course it is. Read this book carefully, and you will

• JOHN P. McCONNELL •

"He had his own magic formula for leadership:

support the managers,

follow up on every issue, keep focused,

and keep it fair.

He understands that if you manage

the people side well, the quality will follow."

see that, although I use the steel industry in many examples, none of what I outline is dependent upon being in the manufacturing business. The system of leadership that I established at Worthington Industries would work for any company. I have no doubt about that.

☞

GRAY IS GOOD

I have never been a black-and-white person. I don't see the world in absolutes. When you care about people as much as I do, you understand how many variables exist for every decision made. It amazes people that I'm not black-and-white in my thinking. They assume that a CEO of a steel company is a hard-nosed man who believes in "my way or the highway." On the contrary, I truly value the trait in myself that allows a bit of gray into every discussion. I am comfortable making decisions without 100% proof one way or another, and every good leader should be. I don't mind when a discussion ends with a split decision among the group members; I have enough confidence and common sense to fill in the gray and make a good decision. The higher I went and the larger the company grew, the less obvious were the decisions that faced me every day, and I was OK with that. Good leaders are comfortable with ambiguity. They have enough faith in themselves to allow gut instinct to fill in the gaps.

Earlier in this book, I explained how I avoided basing decisions on financial statements alone. To me, numbers are a reflection of the past, not a good indicator of the future, and I never expect numbers to tell the entire story. I appreciated having employees who came to me with cut-and-dried analyses on why one decision would be more profitable than another. That was their job. However, each decision I made as CEO also took into consideration the impact on employees, customers, shareholders, and suppliers. Some people, especially from the financial field, were uncomfortable with the gray areas I created, but I reminded them that the role of the CEO is to not trust numbers too much.

My affinity for gray areas also worked well when relating to employees. I recognized that every person in my company had a different story. Not one rule could be written that would take into consideration the broad range of people who worked for Worthington Industries. To look at your employees as one mass of a work force is unfair, and to expect black-and-white decisions when it comes to people is unrealistic. Over the years, I found that the best supervisors are those who could weigh every situation on its own merit, consult the "book of rules," then allow the gray area to creep into the decision. Whether supervisors were purchasing equipment that would help solve a problem or allowing an employee to have extra time off for a family emergency, those who didn't always go by the book were some of our most-respected, productive managers. People wanted to work for them, and they wanted to work *hard* for them.

While most of us think that left-brained workers like accountants and engineers have a hard time with gray areas, I have seen quite a few exceptions over the years. Employees with the combination of detailed minds, confident personalities, and empathetic hearts are an excellent addition to any staff.

From all the CEOs whom I have met over the years, I can say unequivocally that those who can work with "gray" do a better job leading their companies. The qualities on the "softer" side of business, such as fairness, consideration, loyalty, and gratitude, are virtues worth holding, yet they cannot be measured on a pie chart. These virtues can make the difference between a short-lived, profit-driven company and one that will last for generations. The "gray" companies prosper because the human spirit is allowed to live.

• MICK McDANIEL •

"You can't get an argument out of him. He doesn't see
a need for it, because his mind is made up and further
argument is a waste of time. As decisive as he is,
John also is exceptionally softhearted, and sometimes
puts himself in unusual situations because of it. It has
worked for him. I have never heard any employee say
a bad word about him. That's not something any
other CEO I know can claim."

☞

OVERCOME WHATEVER
STIFLES YOUR BUSINESS

Consistency is sometimes hard for larger corporations to maintain because so many factors creep into the mix. Government interferes. Union organizers arrive at your shop to test the waters. New employees come on board who are not as educated in the Three R's as they once were. All of these outside influences can stifle growth, and the CEO's role is to continue slogging through the mud that is thrown in his or her path to lead the company through the mess.

I already have discussed unions enough in this book. Over the years, I also have shared my views with many groups that government must stop being antagonistic to business. America was built with a spirit of innovation, ideas, and risk-taking. That spirit shouldn't be stifled. Legislation will gradually snuff out imagination, innovation, and efficiency. I'm pretty tired of feeling that no good deed shall go unpunished.

Government seems to be following John F. Kennedy's belief that all businessmen are SOBs. This antagonistic approach has saddled American businesses with an administrative burden and costly programs that produce little or no benefit. Hundreds of millions of dollars are spent annually administering and reporting programs mandated by Congress. Most companies far exceed the legislated requirements in healthcare and retirement benefits for employees; still they must file reams of reports. Billions of dollars are spent annually on requirements of the U.S. Environmental Protection Agency. Certainly, we all want clean air and water; however, does it seem logical at all to require businesses to correct problems they did not create? Why should the private sector be forced to clean up a dumpsite that was perfectly legal 20 years ago? What if all laws and regulations were enforced retroactively?

Then there's our educational system. It has strayed from its calling. The Three R's approach that worked well for two centuries of American children gave us the foundation to produce engineering and manufacturing geniuses. Yet, that method of teaching seems to be out of favor today. Our educators must compete with our global economic competitors if we are to remain a world power. Thanks to freedom of the press and advances in technology, we probably have the best-informed work force, but we are far from the best-educated.

If all we had to do as CEOs was run our company in isolation without the outside economic, governmental, and societal factors, our jobs would be so much easier. Obviously, that's not a luxury we have. By building a strong philosophical foundation for your company, relying on your people, and paying attention to your customers, you can go far. But to survive in America today, CEOs also must recognize and address outside forces. They must not be afraid of speaking out on public policy. While most of the people in your company have a very specific job to do, the job of a leader isn't specific. Yes, the size of the job can be overwhelming at times, but you have earned a leadership role for a reason: Because you *can* handle formidable issues. Don't let your followers down.

☞

RECOGNITION IS NUMBER ONE

Allow me to return to the discussion of Recognition. Enough can't be said about it. If you have read this far in my book and still don't see the need to appreciate every individual in your company for the contributions each person makes to your bottom line, then you best start over. Go back to page one.

Everything I have discussed, from coffee breaks to organizational charts, can be boiled down into one lesson: Build a company for the people and by the people, and you'll have a company that reaps rewards beyond your wildest dreams.

To think that you and your small team of managers have all the

• TOM PETERS •

excerpt from <u>Thriving on Chaos</u>

"In fact, John McConnell of Worthington Industries
calls his firm's generous incentive programs 'just one
more form of recognition.' So it is, then, the coupling
that counts: involvement is important."

answers is an absurd notion. To think that you can get the best work or ideas out of people whom you treat as sub-human is preposterous. If you don't do this already, start looking in the eyes of everyone who is contributing to your bottom line, from the man who runs the loudest machine on the night shift to the receptionist who greets all of your customers. What you'll see are other human beings, not machines, who have helped you arrive. They have done your bidding, now do some of theirs.

Recognition of employees is the Number 1 motivator, not money or titles. All employees, even your VPs, are happiest when they feel they are part of the family. In recent years, the shortage of nurses has been a major concern of hospitals throughout the nation. I suggest that one of the major reasons fewer men and women are entering this profession is because nurses are not treated as part of the medical team. Their time on the job is often abused, and their skills are misused. They are paid hourly, while doctors and administrators are not. Rarely are they thanked, except by patients.

Don't let this become a pattern in your company.

A Few Final Thoughts

FINAL THOUGHTS

At Worthington Industries, we have never worked to be big. Rather, our aim has always been to be the best. We strive for quality, and size takes care of itself. We take pride in the fact that our customers tell us we are the best at what we do. Our employees earn above-average income. And the often-forlorn investor has been rewarded, too.

Here's how I would summarize my leadership style:

- *My style is old-fashioned, in the sense that fads and trends have no place in my mode of operation.*

- *My style is simple, in the sense that consistency and respect are the two overriding attributes, and those are not hard to come by.*

- *My style is transferable, because anyone can do it. I held the same philosophies when I ran a five-person shop as when I had thousands of employees. Some of my mentors were successful in the service industry, while I made this work well for manufacturing.*

- *My style is time-consuming. It's not for the CEO who wants to make a quick fix and move on. To connect with employees, to communicate with supervisors, to seek counsel from the management team, to find the best answers when gray areas are acceptable … it all takes time and patience. Perhaps more than anything, it takes a belief that the Golden Rule applies to everyone, not just the privileged or the most profitable — everyone!*

OUR GOLDEN RULE:
THE RIGHT THING TO DO

What a fulfilling life I lead. So many good people have come my way to be part of building one of the strongest companies in the nation.

I don't wonder how I will be remembered. That doesn't matter to me. What has made this whole journey worthwhile is that the way we have led Worthington Industries for 50+ years is, plain and simple, the right thing to do.

THE COLUMBUS BLUE JACKETS

In November 1996, John H. McConnell first submitted an application to the National Hockey League, requesting them to consider Columbus for an expansion team. The application was made by a group of investors calling themselves Columbus Hockey Limited. In June 1997, the announcement came that Mr. McConnell's community would, indeed be given a franchise. While Mr. Mac has always been closely involved in the operations of the Blue Jackets, he hired Doug MacLean in February 1998 to be the man who would build this new team. In September 2000, the Blue Jackets took to the ice in their first pre-season game.

The contribution the Blue Jackets make as an entertainment venue receives more news coverage than the good work the team, staff and supports do off the ice. In March 2000, the Columbus Blue Jackets established the Columbus Blue Jackets Foundation. This grant-making, 501(c) 3, public charity uses the unique resources of its professional athletes, coaches and staff to help improve the quality of life throughout the community. The Foundation donates time, resources, and financial support to organizations committed to meeting the educational, cultural, health and wellness needs of people throughout Central Ohio. A primary focus of the Foundation is the "Stick with Kids" initiative from which a percentage of the annual proceeds is designated for the development of youth hockey. Each year, 75% of the proceeds are redistributed to the community through grants. The remaining 25% serves the cause of youth hockey development.

"With my son now running the daily operations of the company, and me serving as owner of the Columbus Blue Jackets, I am relishing a whole new era of leadership. I completely enjoy the thrill that a sports team brings to my life. In the business world, I never experienced the wide range of emotions that I feel with our very public win-loss record. The sports writers can be brutal. Professional agents can be exasperating. But it's all new to me, and I feel young again."

- MR. MAC

OUR
GOLDEN
RULE